LIVING
WITH
GOD

. . . in Good Times
and Bad

LIVING
WITH
GOD

. . . in Good Times
and Bad

JOHN CARMODY

A Crossroad Book
The Crossroad Publishing Company
New York

1996

The Crossroad Publishing Company
370 Lexington Avenue, New York, NY 10017

Copyright © 1996 by John Carmody

Printed in the United States of America

Library of Congress Cataloging-in-Publication Data

Carmody, John, 1939–
    Living with God— in good times and bad / John Carmody.
      p. cm.
    ISBN 0-8245-1541-2
    1. God—Attributes. 2. Suffering—Religious aspects. I. Title.
BT130.C37 1996
231.7–dc20
                                         95-43605
                                         CIP

FOR ROSEMARY HAUGHTON

Contents

Preface

This small book suggests how we ought to live with God. Such a venture is bold, perhaps even overweening. Who am I to suggest how anyone else ought to live with God? How can any human author, other than an accredited saint, be so audacious?

Aware of these questions, I have yet stumbled on because I have wanted to think about God publicly. Moreover, two books that I have brought out recently — *How to Handle Trouble* (Doubleday, 1993) and *Cancer and Faith* (Twenty-Third, 1994) — have earned me some thanks. So on good days I have thought that perhaps we poor creatures can help one another make a little sense of suffering and God. Perhaps our efforts are not a complete waste. I hope this proves true here, for the venture of this book.

My thanks to all who have encouraged me to keep on, especially my wife, Denise. They have made me think that my terminal cancer need not be without some use — no small gift.

Introduction

GOD

"God" is a small word, yet few human utterances can make a larger difference in life. If you believe in God, you think, or at least hope, that life makes sense. If you do not believe in God, you probably doubt that it does. "Sense," of course, is much in the soul of the beholder. Where one person sees only chaos, another may write God a blank check. Where some members of a support group for cancer patients find little reason to keep going, others continue to think that God is guiding them by the hand.

In the next chapter, when I deal with ways to think well of God, I shall note that God is both personal and impersonal — both a "he" or "she" and an "it." Here, at the beginning, I am thinking of God personally. For example, God is someone involved in the drama, the horrible tragedy, of my friend's lymphoma.

God has been my help in ages past. I hope that God will be my hope for years to come. As I child I learned that all human helps are fragile. As an adult I realize that much of what we understand "God" to be comes from our own projections. However, neither what I experienced as a child nor what I realize as an adult has disenchanted me. On the contrary, God has become different from all human helps — more fascinating. In addition, I keep finding God to be both patient and credible. The otherness of God, the goodness, shows in his always standing by, willing to listen.

I suppose that this is a peasant faith, a theology bowing little to sophistication. So be it. God would not be much help if we could not treat her simply. Yes, it is important to retain a proper awe. Certainly, God remains the one who flung the stars to their corners, who makes the nuclear particles explode. Still, if we are to deal with God well, we cannot let awe paralyze us. God is our salvation only when we can laugh deep in our souls. God is the parent the Bible describes only when we can crawl into her bed and sleep soundly.

Perhaps the first thing to say about God, then, is that we ought to be simple but not simpleminded. God can be both this and that — both near and far, both personal and impersonal. Good theologians do not like either/or. Good theologians prefer both/and. We never finish with God. Always, there is more to say, and more to deny. We shall never understand God. We may say that Native Americans, or traditional Asians, or medieval Muslims created beautiful ceremonies for dealing with God. We have to deny, though, that any of these ceremonies, or all of them added together, produced the last word.

God, in fact, goes before the most creative leaps of our minds, and we find God sitting on the step, waiting patiently, whenever we return to ourselves. God gives us our mental horizons, the lines of light that stretch forth to the unknown. God also causes the inkiest darkness, the fathomless pool in the center of our soul. We can say that "God" entails much of what we experience as "spirit," but we can also feel that God is as solid as the food in our bellies, as thick as the most primal matter. God is a rock as well as a breeze. God is an ocean as well as a thought.

There is no reason not to imagine God as colorful — gold, blue, the incomparable purple of the rarest dawn. Equally, there is reason to think that God lives beyond color, and beyond sound, and beyond texture. God can be nubby, pebbly, rough, but also smoother than silk, sweeter than chocolate, subtle as water, and not perceivable by any sense. This variety can take religious people out of themselves: "O God, how great you are, how wonderful! I love you. If nature and culture did not thrust you upon me, I would think you up. Without you, I would not be. I am myself most when I bow before you, when your love strokes my soul."

Sometimes we have to complain to God. Living toward God, with God, for God can be painful. We never understand what God is up to. We never know for sure where we stand. Being entranced with God makes us eccentric, a puzzle to even our friends. God does not give us money, and God can take away our health. Usually, though, God holds us in a peace more precious than rubies. Yes, sometimes the bottom falls out, but usually God holds us.

There is no one, no thing, like God. God is unique, the only One. Yet God is as modest as a cut flower, as shy as a spring breeze. God gurgles toothlessly in infants. God screams in victims of war. God is in everything, and God is no thing. When we deal with God well, we lose much illusion, and we can gain a wisdom beyond words.

DEALING WITH GOD

More than ten years ago I knew a man with good prospects. He had a job that he enjoyed, that he did well, and that gave him an adequate living. His wife was tall, beautiful, and good. His children had problems, but no more, apparently, than the children of his neighbor a block over, of his colleague two offices down. Then he moved away from where we were both living, and I lost track of him.

One day a mutual friend brought his name up, likening him to Job. He had lost his job. His marriage had blown apart. One of his children had been battered in a bad car accident. Another had been hospitalized for depression. Perhaps worst, lately he had found himself unable to concentrate, as though his short-term memory were going. After inconclusive tests, a neurologist told him that he had the early symptoms of Alzheimer's disease. There was nothing to do but wait and watch.

I contacted this man, got back in touch, because I thought any support his friends could offer had to help. He struck me as broken — unable to focus his mind. When I hung up the phone I realized that my own problems had shrunk markedly. I also realized that the religious faith he and I shared offered few specific explanations. I could not tell him why a wrecking ball had broken his life apart. Living far from him, I had no advice about where he might find a new job, how he might patch up his marriage, what he ought to say to his kids, how he ought to think about losing his mind. I could only tell him of my sorrow, show him my willingness to let him vent some of his frustrations, and commend his plight to God.

Why, though, should I, or he, have to commend his plight to God? Would not a God worthy of the name already know his plight, down to the last detail? Would not a good God already be at work helping him? Indeed, why had not the God in whom he and I trusted warded off his problems, protected him from ever having had to go through such suffering in the first place? These questions, all too familiar from many years spent trying to make sense of faith and suffering, set my head spinning. I knew that I would never answer them. I was sure that the comforts available in the book of Job or the cross of Christ were more emotional than intellectual. They could help me feel that neither my friend nor I was alone in our pain, but they would not explain why any human being had to suffer, let alone why history had included so much evil.

Several years ago I found myself visiting most afternoons in local hospitals. Two good friends were dying of colon cancer, and both seemed to enjoy my visiting them. One liked to talk about death and God and heaven. The other preferred to carry on the kind of conversation we had enjoyed before he took sick, which roamed over novels and politics and music. Both friends weakened steadily, week after week, forcing me to think about death almost constantly.

As I thought, I got no answers, no sure sense of why human beings have to die. My friends were courageous, so I got wonderful lessons in realism, but it was always clear that there were strict limits to what I could understand of their experience. They had been taken to another country, a land of mind and heart to which I was a foreigner. Since the days when I spent so much time visiting my friends in the hospital I have myself stepped into the land of the dying, but only far enough to recognize why my friends did not waste time trying to explain what was happening.

The knowledge that the dying gain is rounder, wholer, than anything they can divide into ideas or serve up to their friends in clear images. They are learning to accept their mortality, to say yes to the necessity that they die, and this learning is very bodily. The pain in their gut, and the morphine that lessens it, and the peculiar blend of clarity and spaceyness that the morphine puts into their head, and the weariness that more and more takes possession of them — these are the lessons, the teachers, that prepare the dying to die. Even had my friends found the words to name these experiences, I could have grasped only a small portion of their import. They were moving along a learning curve unfamiliar even to their doctors, familiar only to other people in the grip of terminal illness.

The sort of knowledge that we gain through terminal illness, as through other primal experiences, is the sort that we need if we are to deal well with God. It is, by the same token, the sort of knowledge that dealing with God, being patient with life's mysteriousness, tends to inculcate in us. Certainly, there are volumes and volumes that can be said about God, as our libraries testify. Some of those volumes are brilliant; many others are full of blather; but that God is in part an intellectual matter seems to me beyond dispute. Equally, however, I find it beyond dispute that none of our volumes removes the mysteriousness of God. As a venerable Christian maxim puts it, "If you have understood, it is not God."

So, in "dealing" with God you have to try for more than understanding, in the sense of clear and distinct ideas. You have to try for something closer to love, the almost carnal knowledge that comes from living with another person — sleeping with your nose in her hair, eating her leftover toast. We should live with God as with a lover or a member of the family — the uncle in the attic, the child with the gap-toothed grin. Sure, God is "infinite" and a lot of other big words. God goes fishing beyond the galaxies and conducts the angels with a golden baton. But God is also my friend, and my amour, and the deadly cancer eating away at my bone marrow. God works in all aspects of my life, every cranny and nook and cell, though I do not know how or why. Otherwise, God is pathetically less than the great deal her name implies.

GOOD TIMES

"Bless the Lord, O my soul, and do not forget his blessings each and all." If I have good times in my memory, I can relate them to God. Weaving my way through them, constructing a narrative, I can think of a history of salvation, a pattern through which God has again and again drawn my life forth from the pit. That is how the Psalmist likes to think, to the praise of God's name. That is how the Bible generally reasons, through a selective rehabilitation of memory.

I remember the first time I saw my sister, when my parents

brought her home from the hospital. I was eight and probably wondering whether I was about to be displaced, but from the moment I pushed aside the blanket and saw her tiny fingers and nose, I was charmed completely. I just wanted to watch her splay those little fingers, wrinkle that tiny nose. She was the smoothest, most beautiful thing I had ever seen. If someone had given me the word, I would have called her a "miracle." Over forty-five years later, something of that initial wonder still lingers.

I also remember a moment ten years after that, when my soul became flooded with light. I was walking in the woods around a little lake, in the squishiness of early spring. My mind emptied, and I stopped worrying about the future. Everything was clear, though nothing was definite, and I knew instinctively that I should abide in this feeling, wait upon the light as long as it stayed. I had arrived, or been taken to, wherever human beings are trying to go when they venture after the meaning of their lives. More than thirty-five years later, I can still reproduce a little of the complete contentment I felt then. Sometimes I think that my most creative work has been an effort to find that lake again.

In good times, we feel supported by a positive mystery of being. Our spirits seem to rest on an updraft of air or a buoyant column of water. We rejoice in existing, convinced that life is good, time is unfolding for our blessing. The words of the poets, the lovers, the beneficiaries of good fortune feel right on our tongue. We have a baby sister or a daughter, and she is extraordinary. God is in our soul, and all is right with the world. These are not illusions. They do not come from a cruel demon, lifting us up so that next week he can dash us down. They are transitory, like all our feelings, but they actually occurred, and they will never not have been.

It is useful to remember the good times, the peak experiences of our lives, as accurately as possible. It is also useful to be grateful for them. We were happy, surprised by joy, and that joy remains instructive. It is good for us to be happy. The accord that joy strikes in our spirit is a primal harmony, telling us about the music of the spheres. Certainly, time tends to chasten our romanticism. We learn that anything like pure joy is an uncommon occurrence. But it would be churlish, even pathological, to disparage the best times of our lives. It would be profoundly wrong only to suspect them — to doubt that human nature can ever simply be right. They tell us volumes about God, though of course much less than the whole story. It is characteristic of God to enter the good, healthy spirit gently, suavely, sweetly, drawing it into light and peace. It is characteristic of the enemy of our welfare, the noxious potential working on us, to upset the good, healthy spirit, treating it violently, with abuse.

If you have ever dealt with a scrupulous person, you know how important this distinction can be. Scrupulous people not only know no peace: they are in danger of destroying the mechanism, the gyroscope, by which alone they could ever find peace. They search for certitudes, proofs that God loves them, or has forgiven them, or is happy with their work. But they are doomed to fail because nothing about God ever becomes certain or patent, exempting us from the need to trust God in faith. We cannot bring a lawsuit against God or wear down God's resistance like a tax accountant. We have to gather ourselves as best we can and hand it all over, messy at the corners. We have to ask God to forgive us for being as we are, creatures bruised, limping, and ugly. This is how God made us, what we were in his mind's eye from the beginning. The bruised reed he will not break. The smoking flax he lets keep smoking.

Perhaps the best of our times with God, the most human, are those when we reach this resigned mood or state of soul. What will be will be — we have simply to trust that God will make it be well. If God should count iniquities, which of us could survive? If this comfortable moral weariness is an illusion, we don't have an ice cube's chance in hell. God has to want the life of the sinner, not her death. If we, evil as we are, know how to give our children good things, how much more God? So we take courage and ask God for bread. We let the staggering audacity of the saints be our guide and lay ourselves down to sleep like nursing children. The love of God becomes prodigal. We dream of the fatted calf, rings on our fingers and bells on our toes. We were lost, but God can find us, whenever God wishes. God can raise up children of faith from stones, turning the hardest hearts to flesh.

There is a gift of tears relevant at this point. The best of our times make our eyes glisten. The goodness of God is more than what our hearts can contain, so our eyes overflow. We cannot say precisely why we are crying. We still have problems and pains and sins. But for the moment they do not matter. For the moment only God matters, and God is only good. This is not a disposition we can create at will. Its coming and going lies out of our hands. But the more habitually we deal with God fully honestly, the more frequently it tends to happen. The more patiently we wait upon God, lamenting but then putting a finger across our lips, the better we can follow Elijah to the mouth of the cave and hear God's still small voice.

BAD TIMES

Once, on a strange planet in a distant galaxy, a woman lied to me, and in consequence made me an utter fool. I believed her when she said she loved me, but it turned out she was bent from the cradle, a liar and a mother of lies. I remember the flush of shame rising from the base of my neck to the ends of my hair. She laughed mockingly, an ugly metallic sound I heard every night for months. My mind said to forget it — laugh it off, take a good lesson in humility, move on sadder but wiser. But my mind was ineffective. Indeed, perhaps the most painful thing I learned was how little love comes under reason. Whenever that woman laughed, part of me died.

Another woman, from a different planet, made me think that God can be an assassin. On a bitterly cold day in January, she buried her husband and with him her soul. Nature itself was lamenting. I have never seen a funeral day more bleak. For the next year, every time I saw her I remembered the funeral. She was six different shades of gray. I never knew teeth could become gray, lips and hands and eyes. Her spirit was gray, her words and rare bits of laughter. Mourning did not become Electra. Mourning became love rubbed beyond raw to gray. I wondered whether the woman regretted her fidelity. Was there any free space in her soul where she might be having second thoughts, wishing she had not made herself so vulnerable? Persistently, I refused to compare her with the first woman, the congenital liar, except to note how rosy were the cheeks of the latter.

In the chemotherapy room, when the talk turns to wigs, I try to lose myself in a magazine, but I still hear three levels of suffering. The most poignant is the deepest, the echoes of feeling ashamed.

Those come from the women who hate caring what cancer is doing to their looks and yet cannot stop themselves. They are strong, and they are petty, and they know exactly the fault line running between the two. Many of them continue to be pretty, though probably they cannot see it. They remind me of paintings from the Low Countries, their colors muted and murky but still pleasing. Above all, they seem tired, weary down to the fine point of their soul. Sometimes they fall asleep to the slow, steady drip of the intravenous line. I like to think they never dream of losing their hair.

When I was in the hospital, not dreaming much myself, the funniest and most disturbing fellow patient would sometimes pierce the predawn with shouts that her bed was on fire. It was a king-size mattress, laid on the floor to accommodate her great bulk. God knows when she had lost her directionals, clearly not just the week before, but each time she erupted in the darkness I came awake with a racing heart. That would quiet easily enough, but sometimes I would begin thinking about losing my own grip on things.

What sort of neighborhood do the senile inhabit? What travel agents book what kinds of trips? A drug such as Demerol can give you a preview, a weekend cruise to Lalaland. There were hours when I did not know whether I was waking or sleeping, times when I was not sure whether I was speaking my words out loud or only chanting them mentally to myself. In lucid moments, I made myself face the sacrifice of my reason. Could I say that for that case, too, what would be would be and let it?

There are more species of bad times than human beings ought to have to know. A man loses his job, and worry begins gnawing at his whole family. A woman finds another lump in her breast, and the dread rises once more. A child looks at the large clock on the corner, which has moved to 5:10. No longer can he deny that his father is late, and as soon as he admits this he must admit the corollary: probably his father has begun drinking again. A very pretty girl, thin to the point of suspicion, asks for an extension on her paper. Why does she need it? the innocent instructor asks. Tonelessly, she replies that her neck is not responding to therapy, and so she is in constant pain. The instructor should know better, but his innocence is two parts stupidity, so he keeps plowing ahead. What is the matter with her neck? The girl gazes at him so levelly he might be a red light: when she was small and would cry, her mother used to bang her head on the floor. That injured her neck permanently.

No bad time is purely physical or purely emotional, as is no good time. Her pain in the neck would be less if the girl did not have to wonder whether she was not a hypochondriac. People who have cancer may manage the emotional swings quite well and still suffer racking muscle spasms or violent vomiting. Yes, in the midst of the worst times, seasons of peace and grace can blow in. But that is not the prevailing pattern. The prevailing pattern is for pain to bring with it depression.

Depressed, in pain, we inevitably become patients. We are suffering, forced to endure things that should not be, sent on a terrible journey. Fortunate as our life may have been previously, it is now a crucifixion. We have become people of sorrow — despised, rejected, acquainted with grief. The better our religious preparation, the more we deal with this grief before God.

There are no accidents in God's creation. God is responsible for the plan, the providence, by which the world runs. We did not choose the genes responsible for our cancer. We did not make the virus that came out positive in our test for HIV. God is the maker of heaven and earth, genetic codes and viruses. On God's head let them be. God was happy to give us the light of our eyes and the air we breathe. We were right to sing God psalms of pure praise. We can be equally right, in our crucifixion, to accuse God of abandoning us, as long as we listen for God's reply.

In good times and bad, we are wise to listen. God seems to reply often, though seldom in words. The gray woman who haunts my memories of funerals somehow got through the first year, after which she got back some color. The little boy who felt his heart sink as he watched the large clock reach 5:10 learned to walk down to the next corner for the 5:20 bus, though the first few times he was crying. It wasn't fair, he and the gray woman agreed. It should not have been that way. But it was, and it got a little better when they faced it. They didn't like crying, but if crying helped, they would cry and cry some more. For they knew, like wounded animals, that they could only curl up and wait for healing. I think such waiting can be the marrow of prayer.

THIS BOOK

This book concerns dealing with God, in good times and bad. Inevitably, therefore, it has a lot to say, and even more to imply, about prayer. For even when I am discussing how to think about God, or feel about God, or share a given time with God, or choose to give God carte blanche, I am wanting to bring God before you: summon the mystery as prayer does, so that divinity can speak for itself. Correlatively, I am wanting you to listen to the mystery as though you were praying — to the God who is as close as a basic question, never farther away than a good thought.

Why is there something rather than nothing? How does it happen that the sun rises each morning and that every child born of woman dies? Do not, I pray you, dismiss simple questions such as these. Distinguish yourself from the cows in the paddock. Do not run away in confusion or fear or irritation. It is good for thoughts such as these to confuse you, right and helpful to your salvation. They are in fact very gentle. The God who sends them knows the weakness of your frame, the misery of your education.

This is a book about spiritual education. It concerns the development of your soul. It does not treat you as the newspapers do. It does not despise you, dumb things down to you, as television does. It thinks of you as a friend because it knows that you are a fellow-sufferer and that our world is racked by injustice and disease. You have gone through some painful times, and you have the scars to show for them. What have those times taught you? Less, in all likelihood, than they should have. Probably you have yet to let go of some key illusions. I find mine slow to leave. Probably you still imagine that things or moods or human relations can fulfill you or keep you safe. Very human, but not very wise.

Nothing can keep you safe. You are flesh and so always vulnerable. You are mortal, bound to die, and so can wake terrified any night. On the other hand, you are also spirit, and so, if you wish, you can think your way to a measure of freedom, even over against death. You can love and so be purified gradually by suffering toward wisdom, even holiness. Life is not safe. Time is not safe. Death is certain, and eternity is not. This is your situation. Your task is to make the most of it. At its core, pulling all the strings, is God. If you wish, God can move you toward peace.

God is the sole reality that is radically different, adequate. All the rest — rocks, trees, tigers, human beings, angels, clouds — get their definition from God. They are all limited. Only God is limitless. (Only the ignorant think of God as limited, though the ignorant can gain academic degrees and write heavy books.) Created things all change, come and go, while God always remains. God is there in the morning, when you first open your eyes. God beds down with you at night, as you slip into sleep for relief. So omnipresent, God could be a tyrant, Job's cruel watcher-of-men. However, if you wish, God can become present everywhere as your rock and our salvation, your lover who never fails.

In this book I hope to show how God might become your lover who never fails. It is a quixotic venture, bound to miscarry, but I love to put my mind to it, my heart, soul, and strength. For by thinking about how to think about God, how to sift through typical feelings about God, how to work for God, and how to love God, I can feel my spirit move toward the still point, the center that just might hold. Even to glimpse that center, for a moment admire its matte finish, is reward enough for my labor.

Anyway, God is in your life, whether you like it or not. For better of worse, richer or poorer, you are involved with more than you can understand, a genuine mystery. You do not know where you came from, regardless of how detailed a genealogy you obtained from Salt Lake City. You do not know where you are going. No medium or palmist can show you. The more you know about evolution, the more impressed you are likely to be. The physical development of life boggles the mind, intimates far more than any single brain can hold. The more you know about human history, especially its cruelties, the likelier you are to find human nature both opaque and frightening. You cannot know the person next to you at the supper table, even the person staring back from the mirror. On days when your hormones dip the whole world can become strange, fuzzy, and out of kilter. Already you know, even if you are not old, that many days you do well just to keep going, just to avoid cracking up.

I believe that dealing with God well can help you keep going and that it can patch up your inevitable cracks. In this book I am out to offer ideas and images and calls to feeling that make plain human existence, ordinary lives like yours and mine, mysterious in the most positive sense. There is more, always and everywhere, than we can understand. Therefore, always and everywhere there are grounds for thinking that, just possibly, tomorrow may be better than a terrible today.

In this work I use the traditions about God, Eastern and Western, to bring such grounds for hope into language and focus. I deny that the world religions exhaust what "God" can mean, and I agree that often religious people have been despicable — crusaders serving anything but God. I think it stupid, though, to ignore the world religions, because despite their sins they have stored away most of what the best and brightest human beings have created in our one hundred thousand years or so of history. For the art of being human, the consummate adventure of probing the mystery of life to the maximal degree possible, the world religions, the main traditions about God, stand without peer. Come and see.

Chapter One

Thinking about God

OVERVIEW

The basic sense of God in this book is "mystery." God is the fullness of reality, the limitlessness of implication and possibility, suggested by the unimaginable reach of the universe, the endless play of our minds. I assume that God is always with us. As soon as we think, imagine, love — exercise any of our human capacities — we summon, depend upon, and enter into the mysteriousness of God. We human beings are the species that lives self-consciously, reflexively, toward a horizon that can be unlimited. Our science, art, politics, sports, religion, and all the rest spring from this capacity, this intercourse with mystery, expressing it and modifying it.

Therefore, "God," as I use the term, is an ingredient in what it means to be human, what we denote when we refer to thought. Therefore, God is objective — as real as Mount Rushmore, as daunting and unavoidable as the budget deficit. God lies at the foundations of personalities that are strong but just as surely at the foundations of personalities that are weak. Poetic people may summon better language for God than people who are prosaic, but prosaic people may deal with God better, be more impressive saints. There is no life without God. The fierce atheist has more to do with God than the sleepy believer.

All our images for God, all our thoughts and feelings, all our strategies, including the admirable one of staying still, come up short of the objective, living, unavoidable reality. We cannot get our minds around God. We cannot get our hearts fully in touch with God. God does not submit to our feelings, though "God" tends to provoke the best of our emotions (and perhaps also the

25

worst). We never understand God, but sometimes we can feel God's presence. God deals with us as a lover, a friend, a gentle parent, a stern judge. God also ignores us as the clouds do, rolls over us like the wind and the rain. We are born miraculously, the result of processes at which only the most obtuse of us do not gape. We die without knowing why or whereunto. In between these two terminals we experience pleasure and pain, failure and success, good days, bad days, days indifferent. In all this summary religious experience we are more like our neighbors, both near and far, than unlike them. In all this bedrock human endurance our being male or female, rich or poor, black or white, modern or prehistoric is secondary.

Throughout what we know of human history, all peoples have tried to make sense of the mysteriousness of their situation. In every era and locale, both women and men have told stories, drawn pictures, sung songs, and danced dances to express their intuitions of how they might cope best. In this first chapter I look at how we tend to create images of God, what some of the most important impersonal images for God have been, and how some of the most important personal images might still serve us well today.

Specifically, in the next section I describe *icons* — sacred images that religions tend to create for God. This topic allows us to study the imaginative processes at work in typical human thinking about God. It also allows us to study the function of Jesus, the prime Christian icon, in Christian thinking about God (a thinking that has had a great influence in American culture). After dealing with icons, I present four impersonal images for God that have carried great weight historically, especially in Western cultures but also, to a lesser extent, in Eastern cultures. These four impersonal images are *infinity* (God's being boundless, limitless), *light* (both physical and mental), *darkness* (also both physical and mental), and *being and nothingness* (existence as the fullness of reality, but not as a thing, a limited reality or creature). Certainly, we could consider other impersonal images profitably, such as eternity, transcendence, creativity, or even evil. Nonetheless, studying these four will make the main point: God is always more than human.

Four other images for God that I describe are personal, coming from the tendency of many cultures to treat God as though he were a center of intellect and will, understanding and love, imagination and feeling. The four personal images are *Lord, Father and Mother* (parent), *friend,* and *lover.* They have been primary ways in which religious people have brought God to mind, have channeled their intuitions of who God is and how they ought to relate to God. Once again, I forgo studying other significant, interesting, viable images: teacher, Creator, savior, judge, and more. For my main point—which is that human beings are bound often to speak with God, and listen for God, as though he or she were a superperson—these four images of Lord, parent, friend, and lover should suffice.

By the end of the chapter, I hope that the word "God" may make more sense than it did at the beginning. Ideally, you will grasp better what goes into thinking about God and why no single image is adequate. If so, the result will be what some theologians call an "analogical" imagination about God. You will sense, and agree, that God is both like and unlike what we say about God, what we imagine. My own prejudice is to agree with the Fourth Lateran Council (1215) and say that God is more unlike than like what we say or imagine about God. I find it congenial finally to shut down my mind and attend to the divine mystery as a whole, in a wraparound silence. But that need not be your preference. You may prefer to sing psalms or gaze at holy pictures. You should deal with God however you find best. You should think whatever thoughts bring you the most courage, peace, and joy.

ICONS

An icon is a sacred image. It is a picture, physical or mental, that mediates the divine. The people using an icon think that through it they can make contact with God, feel divinity and unite themselves to it. The most famous icons are personal, depicting God or a saint (taken as a human place where God has loved to dwell) as though God has a face, deals with us through mind and heart. However, sacred stones, mountains, rivers, animals, and other impersonal forms or forces qualify as "icons" in the broad sense that I want the word to carry here. Here an icon is simply a material or symbolic presence or focus for the divine. Everywhere human beings use icons so that they can avoid being completely silent, blind, mute, helpless, or hopeless before the mystery dominating their lives. Everywhere the dependence of human thought on imagination means that theology will deal in icons.

On the whole, Eastern religions are prodigal, even promiscuous, with images for the divine. Indian religion (Hinduism especially) often suggests that God is mysterious (that the foundations and ends of existence lie beyond our comprehension) by letting images proliferate wildly and clash. So Indian iconography makes the divine both male and female, both animal and human, both kind and cruel, the source of both life and death. Some schools of Indian thought (both Hindu and Buddhist) prefer negative images, symbols by which they hope to defeat the drive of the mind to make icons, but mainstream Indian religion multiplies icons.

Behind a preference for negative images (in-finity, darkness) tends to lie an awareness that all images are limited and so carry the danger of distorting the simple wholeness of ultimate, divine reality. Thus Indian saints have chanted that God, the ultimate reality, is *neti, neti* (not this, not that). Nothing we can say about God, no images that we can create, do God justice, render the ultimacy of the divine as it deserves. Even so negative an image as the Buddhist nirvana (nothingness, blown-out-ness) is but a useful convenience, becoming dangerous if people take it literally.

East Asian religious symbolism tends to be more concrete than Indian, and East Asians feel most comfortable theologically when closest to nature. Thus Confucian, Taoist, Eastern Buddhist, and Shinto symbols usually subordinate the personal to the impersonal. When depicting the Chinese Buddhist Way or Suchness, or the Shinto *kami* (spirits), these religious systems stress the otherness that nature presents to human beings, its difference from our abstractive, somewhat rational ways.

The great Asian goal, both Indian and East Asian, is harmony, and the primary instance of harmony is human beings' getting along well with nature — avoiding natural disasters, enjoying sufficient fertility in their animals and fields to gain food, shelter, and a minimal sense of safety. To gain such harmony, Asian sages agree, the lesser has to submit itself to the greater, human beings have to subordinate themselves to nature, the seasons and stars.

Some scholars describe Judaism and Islam as aniconic (anti-representational) religions. The passion for the oneness, the overwhelming singularity of the Lord or Allah, that Jews and Muslims worship makes them reject, even hate, any representations of God — animal or human, natural or social. Still, it is impossible for human beings to do without images of some sort. The Jewish "Lord" inevitably calls to mind a king or Creator, even though the rabbis argue valiantly that God is more than either. The same for the Muslim Allah, who is Lord-of-the-worlds, Creator of human beings from a mere clot of blood.

Moreover, both the Lord and Allah are personal, inasmuch as they rule a world they have brought into being intelligently, by the simple exercise of their will. They command the stars, the angels, human beings. The latter come into great peril if they disobey God. God gives them laws and woe betide them if they do not follow God's laws. Jewish Torah (guidance) and Muslim Shariah (law, direction) are complicated sets of images that depend on (a supposition of) the personal willfulness of divinity — on God's having laid out for human beings in detail how they ought to behave.

Both Torah and Shariah depict human existence as a social bond between a people and God — a bond ideally working itself out by the people's living as God's laws prescribe, doing what their holy traditions dictate. Indeed, much of both the Jewish Bible and the Muslim Koran boils down to a presentation of such holy traditions — a description of the sovereign word and will of God.

Christianity is perhaps the most complicated iconographic system among the world religions. The reason is the unique place occupied by its founder. Neither Muhammad, with whom the Muslim era proper begins, nor any of the Jewish founders (Abraham, Moses, David) claimed to be divine or has traditionally been considered divine. Scholars debate whether Jesus himself claimed to be divine, but there can be no denying that for hundreds of years orthodox, fully traditional Christians have considered Jesus to be both divine and human.

Indeed, the canonical (regulative) Christian theology that one finds in the New Testament and early Christian centuries makes Jesus himself the prime icon through which his followers are to worship God. This canonical theology says that Jesus is at one and the same time both fully human and fully divine. He is as much a man, a human being, as any other member of our species — Napoleon, Marie Antoinette. Yet he is also as fully divine as the God to whom he himself prayed (his "Father") and as the

Holy Spirit who guided him. How Jesus can be both fully human and fully divine is not clear, could never become clear. Indeed, Christian theology holds that the union of humanity and divinity in Jesus is a strict mystery, something that human beings have never understood, can never understand. The same for the Christian teaching that God is a Trinity of divine "persons" (unlimited centers of consciousness): Father-Son-Spirit. Jesus is the "incarnation," the enfleshed form, of the second person of this Trinity, the Son or Word. But how he is this, precisely what the words denote, passes beyond human comprehension.

The reasonableness of the faith that these two central Christian doctrines (Incarnation and Trinity) are mysteries stems from the occurrence of divinity in both. Because in Christian theology divinity is by definition unlimited and so for human beings literally not-to-be-comprehended (grasped), both the Incarnation and the Trinity are bound to be mysteries in the strict sense of the term: too much for human beings to comprehend. One cannot understand what Jesus is because Jesus is divine as well as human. One cannot understand how Father-Son-Spirit possess divinity or display it because "divinity" never comes under human control. One can only say that, on the basis of the reported religious language of Jesus himself, Christians have found warrants for developing their trinitarian view of God and their conviction that Jesus himself is the central image of this God. Similarly, one can only say that, on the basis of their traditions about Jesus, which include his death on the cross and strange "resurrection" from the dead, Christians have found warrants for developing their view that in Jesus divinity took flesh and dwelt among us.

My point is neither to discourse at length on Christian theology nor to defend it. My point is simply to explain the core of traditional Christian faith sufficiently to show why iconography has been so central. Because the Christian understanding of God is that in Jesus God became human, without ceasing to be God, orthodox Christians have thought that human flesh in particular, along with material creation in general, is a valid, somewhat trustworthy expression of the divine nature. Summarily, Christians have said that Jesus shows us what God is like in human terms. For Christians, Jesus is the best likeness of the divine that one can get, the most adequate.

Because Jesus is fully human, and so is limited as all human beings are, Jesus does not exhaust what divinity is like, cannot be said to be the only valid icon. However, for traditional followers Jesus is the privileged icon, the one around whom believers are required to arrange all their other images of God. Though characteristically Christian thinkers have agreed with Jewish and Muslim thinkers that God is mysterious, and so that no imagery is ever adequate, they have had to qualify this agreement, inasmuch as they have believed that Jesus is fully divine and so gives divinity a trustworthy human face.

So much, then, for a brief general reflection on how religious people the world over have tended to deal with the matter of representing God. We turn now to four impersonal images that have been important, beginning with infinity.

INFINITY

When I was a boy I spent several summers largely under water. We lived near a lake, so I supplemented my baseball with swimming. Sometimes four or five other kids and I would jump on an inner tube from a large airplane tire and paddle out to deep water. There we would dive off the tube, come up through its hollow middle, and drift on it as though it were HMS *Bounty*.

Other times, which I remember better, I was alone. I would head for the wharf extending out into the lake on barrels, under which I had constructed a magical world. The sunlight would slant down through the wooden planks of the wharf, turning the water varying shades of green. I could hold my breath long enough to swim under all the barrels, or come up under the center ones, or even cruise up under the runway, where there was only six inches or so of water. I could move like a submarine, or a spy, or the champion of a new Olympic event: barrels. I could drift menacingly like a shark, run silent and deep, make not the slightest ripple, attack in elegant fury. It was cool under the wharf, both refreshing and stylish. I delighted in playing there, alone, because it fed my imagination, led me out into endless new worlds. In retrospect, the times I spent under the water those summers were some of the happiest in my childhood. They were also some of the most formative. For under that neighbor's little wharf I learned about infinity. Even today, the endlessness that theology taught me to associate with God laps in my mind like dappled water.

The play that I loved among the barrels, the stimulus to constant inventiveness, primed me to think of the human mind as the medieval philosophers did. Thomas Aquinas, for example, said that the mind is *potens omnia facere et fieri*: able to make and become all things. When religious people speak of human beings as made in God's image, this should be much of what they have in mind. The creativity of little children, maturing in the laboratories of immunologists, the lofts of painters, the late night vigils of poets, is a mark of God. All culture comes from it — literature, music, math. All babble ought to bow to it and cease, as though in the presence of something holy. A major reason that we can think that God is infinite, always able to be or do more, is that our own minds are protean — can mold themselves to this and that, dart here and there, travel on eagles' wings. We can think that God is unbounded because we ourselves can imagine barriers, our climbing over them, and our then painting the shed where they are stored black and yellow for the bumblebees.

The infinity, the unboundedness, of God pleases me immensely. That God has no limit gives me pleasure beyond measure. God goes on and on, way out beyond the nebulae. God goes down and down, to smaller and smaller T cells, proteins, molecular bits of genes. And God does this morally as well as physically. God need not stop at X measure of goodness, Y amount of patience or love. Woe to us, then, if we try to invoke God's name against lesbian mothers, people who chew garlic, or non-Muslims we consider infidels.

We do not know much about God, precisely because there are in God so few limits. God can be nothing evil, nothing cabined, nothing irrational. But we cannot always be certain whether something is evil, or where its joints lie, or what largest sense it is serving. We have to say that God can always exceed our limits, making a dozen new species in a single Ice Age. We have to say that creation may be moving — a process and game God still enjoys. We just do not know, and neither do our opponents. God can go on and on — in time, meaning, goodness, space, dipping down to new planes, bending back, zooming here, there doing barrels and loops.

Suppose that God, like the burning bush of Moses, is a fire

that does not consume. Maybe God burns on and on, a pillar always lighting the night. Or suppose that God is the purest mist, a cloud lovely to both brow and soul. Maybe God moves graciously through the sky, giving shade, cool, and reflection. Limpid, liquid, subtle as water, God may lap at every shore, moving constantly and never ceasing, always flowing, changing, coming home, and taking off. These would be just a few of the ways in which God is in-finite, free of terms, barriers, forms.

To imagine the world we know, even in new forms we have yet to see, we have to blend stability and newness, limits and going beyond. Maybe God likes stability, structures, dependability enough to impose her own limits. Or maybe God quickly tires of limits, itching to be away and make all things new. Or, most likely of all, maybe God is sometimes this and sometimes that, stable today and mercurial tomorrow. With "God" we reach the very edge, the outer banks of how we conceive of reality.

God is the other from which we rebound when we accept barriers of any kind. God is the foundation of the skyscraper going down, down below, well out of sight, but God is also the top far above, lost in the cloud. God is stuff, primordial matériel, but even more God is spirit, primordial immatériel. That is the greatness of God, his evasion of all limits, her status as the first and the last.

In the book of Revelation (21:5) the resurrected Christ says, "Behold, I make all things new." Revelation intuits that his resurrection has rejoined Christ to the first source, the God who is less a warehouse than a nuclear explosion, the sun of suns. In Revelation, Christ is the end as well as the beginning, because unless all things go to him, end up happy in his lap, they are chapters of a tale never finished, a story always maundering on. So the limitlessness beautiful in God becomes grotesque in creatures, trapping them in their incompleteness. Only a mad person — a Hitler, a Pol Pot — tries to make his claim to divinity take hold, cracking apart in the process, creating spasms of bloodshed.

So, a prayer: O God, do not let the thought of you destroy us. Do not let your endlessness break our minds with envy or fear. Help us at the right time to let understanding go, realizing that we can never comprehend you. As death settles into our bones, be our only divinity, the sole maker we accuse, the only holiness upon which we rely. May our love for you make you lovely in the sight of other people, especially those who mourn. May the limitlessness we worship in you make you our absolute future, and theirs as well.

LIGHT

Light is a natural symbol for God. Thus in ancient Egypt the break of day signaled the coming of the sun god Re. Thus in scripture the coming of dawn is like the arrival of a great king on Mount Zion, his revered holy place. The human spirit longs for the light and finds the darkness frightening. In the physical light we can see our way, notice the danger coming. In the light of our minds, the clarity of our spirits, we can think that how we are living makes sense. So scripture (1 John 1:5) says that God is light in whom there is no darkness at all. This divine light is both physical and spiritual.

Recently I watched a family struggling with the man's losing his job. It was unfair, frightening, painful to all of them. The man himself was wounded and suffering. His wife and the children came under a cloud. Whereas a month previously they had been a happy, sunny group, now they were dispirited. Whereas before their problems had been serious but manageable, now their backs and spirits were bent. A light had gone out. A dark mood of worry and trial had blown in. You did not have to be privy to their tabletalk or tears to know that they were suffering. When would their God lighten their days, ease their heavy burdens?

We look to God for light, and we hope that God will give us relief from our burdens. We think of "God" as pure clarity that wishes us well. In the next section, dealing with darkness, we can explore another zone of the divine mystery, where human beings are bound to investigate ways of God that they can neither grasp nor call good easily. Here, though, let us concentrate on the divine light. Here let us gather together the instinct of virtually all peoples, from all places and times, that "light" names something primordial about holiness, something bound to go along with "God."

In heaven, where light seems to predominate, one might find an overview, a comprehensive picture, of what is happening in the world, how all the affairs of nature and human beings are unfolding. A divinity responsible for the world, for hanging the sun and the moon in their places, could see everything from heaven — all would be clear, naked, obvious. And though sometimes we fear this sort of divinity, a God seeing everything that we do, knowing everything that we think, part of us also wants it. For part of us wants *someone* to see everything, know all that is going on, sift out the rewards and punishments. "Light" goes hand in hand with confidence that there is such a someone, that the world does make sense, is not a complete chaos. The family I watched trudging in darkness had to wonder whether their lives had turned upside down, where fairness and meaning had gone.

Between her first and second child, a woman I knew well suffered three miscarriages. She wanted a second child passionately, so each of these miscarriages not only was painful physically but also brought her spirits low. A shadow came over her life for a while, fortunately not too long, until she healed and gained the resolve to try again. This woman was not poor or uneducated or unlucky in other ways. Her first child was healthy and happy, the rest of her family life was fine. Yet she still carries some scars. Looking back from the outside, I think of that time as a period of darkness. The woman might laugh ruefully now, but then the light had dimmed in her eyes, the play and humor lessened. Until she solved the problem (found the infection responsible for the miscarriages), she was sad and her world lacked a glow.

For the past several years, I have been in and out of hospitals, laboratories, and doctors' offices several times each month. Most of these visits have been parts of a routine monitoring of my myeloma, but on occasion something has gone out of kilter more dramatically and created bad news. I'd like to think that I have accepted my physical situation sufficiently to make me relatively impervious to emotional ups and downs. I'd like to think that bad news from laboratories or exams would not depress me. But it can. When it comes, my spirit clouds over, my world loses its glow. In contrast, if further information changes the picture for the better, sunshine breaks through. At least for the near future, the picture is not gloomy. So I thank the God of light for small favors.

We love the God of light instinctively, and we only put up with the God of bad news as best we can. We endure the dark times, with more or less grace, slogging through the puddles, but if those times stretch out for long, we start to wonder why life is treating us badly. True, on the whole we do not demand constant sunshine. We know that most people have to go through dark days, and sometimes we suspect that this is helping our character. But we find it dangerous to associate darkness, misfortune, suffering with God. Such an association can make God seem cruel.

We do not want God to seem cruel. We want God to connote savor and light. For if savor and light go out of God, where in the world shall we find them? The light in ourselves is so small, so beleaguered and frail, that it could never illumine a good life. The darkness spread by the loss of a job, or the return of a cancer, or the breakup of a marriage, or the poverty of the world's masses is too great a burden for us to carry alone.

Little in the challenge of facing the great darkness of human existence is invigorating. Most of it we handle by plain enduring. The emotional support and practical help of friends can be crucial, in good measure because it brings in a little light. But the support of friends is uncertain. Like us, they come from dust, and unto dust they will return. So pain drives us toward the depths of creation, where even unawares we search for a light that darkness has never comprehended.

DARKNESS

We shy away from darkness, instinctively, yet we cannot avoid it, either in our own lives or in how we think about God. Eventually, darkness can become charming and helpful to our dealings with God, but at the outset we tend to find it frightening and so like little children hide under the covers. If, on analysis, "light" turns out to be complicated, nothing so simply transferrable to God as sunshine or the switching on of a bulb, "darkness" turns out to be even more complicated, standing for both the misfortune that can visit any of us and for all the ways in which ultimate issues, including God, are larger than we can understand.

I have alluded to misfortune, describing how clouds come into most lives. The worst of human times, though, bring a darkness thicker than mere cloudiness. The gray woman I mentioned earlier went through a midnight of the soul. The death of her husband created a void, an absence of color and light, that for a year contained her like a prison, even a grave. The reminders I have gotten (from lab reports, literature, and pain) that my myeloma is terminal, surer to bring me a premature death than most other forms of cancer, have sometimes drawn a curtain over the future, making me wonder whether continuing to work, or even continuing to pray, makes any sense.

Any people with dignity try to avoid dramatizing the darkness through which they may be passing. Unless we are completely self-centered, we know that all sorts of other people are also going through hard times, some much worse than ours. Still, we cannot deal with God honestly, nor come to grips with our own emotional needs, unless we are willing to face our darkness straightforwardly, admitting that we are confused, depressed, in pain.

Physical pain is a burden and a darkness, causing many people to debate whether they should crawl out of bed in the morning. Emotional, mental, or spiritual pain — choose what name you prefer — is also a burden and a darkness. Both kinds of pain paint over the skylight through which we like to look at God. Both make it harder to praise the course of the sun through the heavens and keep open a joyous soul.

Still, the personal part of theology, the wrestling of our souls with "God," has a great many positive things to say about darkness, especially the darkness of God. If God is infinite, as we have already mused, then God escapes the confines of our understanding — steps beyond, or always lives beyond, our little light. God in himself or herself or itself can then be "dark" for us simply because we can never see God, grasp God mentally, or know where we stand with God. However, if we can feel and love beyond where or what we can know, and if darkness can suggest this "beyond," then in darkness we may be able to find more of God, and meet God more ultimately, than is possible in light.

These are suggestions, indeed reports of experience, that we find in the writings of the great mystics, East and West. Such mystics have dealt with God nakedly, without the protection of customary images or ideas. God has emptied their hearts and minds, seared their souls. So when they speak of darkness we should listen. When they talk of the need to die to commonsensical or worldly certitudes, so as to be reborn to a more adequate relationship with God, based on abandoning ourselves in trust, we should pay attention.

Certainly, "darkness" will not hand God over to us any more than "light" will, but if we let God show himself, deal with us in both modes, we shall come away the richer. We shall, for example, make our own the commonplace theological assertion that nothing limited, finite, can represent God adequately. We shall also, more subtly, realize one day that God is beyond our feeling as well as our visual imagery, is not limited to either light touches or heavy blows. If we are willing or able, strong enough or brave enough, to hang on in the darkness, keep plodding through the hard times, we can experience, now and then, that hanging on, trying, is the heart of the mystical matter.

We don't have to understand. We don't have to like or feel good about where we find ourselves, how God seems to be coming or going. We just have to agree to it, in the sense of acknowledging that it is so, of saying, "Yes, all right, get on with it," of not denying that darkness is where we, and our God, now seem to be. We may still run away sometimes, out of fear of being overwhelmed. We may still resent our pain, not want God to be so demanding. But if we come back when we can, pick ourselves up and try again, the next time enduring the darkness will be easier. We still will not understand why God should be dark, why life should be painful, but we may feel less panic or scandal. Indeed, if we are people formed by scripture we shall remember the many trials of Israel, and the fate of Christ on the cross. If we read the lives of holy people, we shall find that virtually all of them went through times when they felt abandoned.

The "darkness" of God can stand for all the pain in the fact that the Ultimate in our lives is too much for us. With God we are overmatched — from the outset, through the middle, at the end. The more closely we concern ourselves with God, the more profoundly we are going to suffer from this overmatch. On the other hand, the more we are also going to become reconciled to the fact that darkness is often the way things are, mystery is often unavoidable. And when we accept even momentarily that mystery is often unavoidable, our failure, even our dying, loses much of its horror and edge.

All people die. Most people fail, in one way or another. God defeats everybody, sooner or later, more or less painfully. I have my cancer. You have your lost job. My friend has his divorce and Alzheimer's disease. We are a motley crew, slashed and gasping, sometimes so torn and bandaged as to invite laughter. God is dark for all of us, as for myriads of Africans and Asians, people far away and long ago. But we can get used to this fact. God can work us around.

BEING AND NOTHINGNESS

The last of our impersonal images for God joins two suggestions. God is being — pure, original is-ness. God is also nothingness — not limited in being, not a thing or entity like the others that come to us through our senses and submit to the manipulation of our concepts.

First, God is being. Because of the influence of Indo-European thought in Western theology, being has played an important role in both academic and official views of God. If we think of "creation" as the process through which things come into being, gain reality, God is the Creator because God is the source of being, the one who grants reality to everything that gains it. The stars come from God, and so do the atomic particles. Human beings come from God, and so do pandas and poison ivy. God is the only source of be-ing. If something exists, is real, it is so in virtue of God.

Everything that we experience directly seems limited in its be-ing. It changes, comes into being and passes away, is born or dies. Yes, as long as it exists there is something absolute about its being. It cannot be and not be at the same time, at least under the same aspect. But *what* it is dominates its being. It is only as a lion or a tiger or a stockbroker. It is not absolutely — with no predicate or qualification, no constraint to being only a particular something, a this rather than a that (a Siberian tiger, and so not a Bengal).

When theologians speak of God as being, they want God to have no limitations — not be this or that, have no particular whatness or essence. The only thing orthodox Western theologians shaped by Indo-European studies of being are willing to say about the whatness of God is that what God is is to be. So, for example, Parmenides, a pre-Socratic Greek philosopher, had a vision of being that led him to exclaim, "Is!" It is not clear that Parmenides was speaking of what most religions call God, but it is clear that simple existence, being without limitation to a particular form, had struck him forcibly, so that he cried out as though in worship.

What is this to you and me, simple people trying to deal with God, the mystery at the foundation and center and end of our lives? Well, it can be a way of picturing, thinking about, why we never get a handle on God and yet still suspect regularly that God is fully real. God as being is somewhat like the air, or the light by which we see. The air is just there. Usually we don't pay special attention to it, don't in fact even notice it. We breathe it in, and we must have it to live, but unless there is something wrong with it (it is filthy or too thin or too heavy), it does not concern us. It seems too vague, unformed, general, pervasive to grab our attention.

Few people pay more attention to being than they pay to the air they breathe. Only people exposed to philosophical studies of being or mystical literature are likely to finger mentally the isness of things. Only people who have tried to follow a thinker such as Saint Augustine as he goes down the chain of his own being, his self, in search of what anchors him in existence are likely to think that the isness of God carries great significance for their own lives.

Yet it most certainly does. If it is not clear why any of us should exist or why, more broadly, there has ever been something rather than nothing, then the fact that we do exist makes us the focal point of a mystery, a place touched by God, the source of being. God, then, is as near to us, as closely identified with us, as our being. As long as we take breath, occupy space and time, God is in us, with us, furnishing the isness that keeps us on this side of nothingness, away from the void.

The second part of the imagery of being and nothingness that we are applying to God, the nothingness, invites us to ponder the darkness or seamlessness of pure being. If we agree to call God isness without limit, being that is not restricted to being something, then God is not a thing. "Things" are limited physical realities. God is not limited, and God is not simply physical. Is God then just an idea, a mental thing? No, not that either, because an idea is also limited, is almost always an idea of something — raccoon, isosceles triangle, limited partnership in a mothballs firm. Certainly, we have an idea of God (must have, to talk about God), as we have an idea of being. But in both of these unusual cases the idea turns out to have little content or definition. We don't get a mental picture that allows us to describe God the way we can describe the Metropolitan Museum of Art, or the Old Curiosity Shop, or former mayor Dinkins.

The same with the idea of being. We may picture an amorphous blob, or a blazing light "is-ing" out of the void, or a speculative scene in which new hydrogen atoms somehow emerge out of antimatter. But we remain frustrated if we insist on equating reality with the limits of things, either physical things or mental things (ideas).

So it can be useful to ponder the no-thing-ness of God. God stands before, ahead of, any divisions of reality into thises and thats, and God also stands behind any such divisions. The infinity of God assures God's nothingness. Yes, the word "God" is something, a puff of air standing for an idea, a three-letter unit when it comes to spelling. But the reality toward which the word "God" points is not a something. It is closer to an everything, a whole, an All.

The great philosophical puzzle is not how there can be a God but how there can be realities less than God — creatures, beings that are finite, that come and go. As unlimited God can always have been. As not a thing, in no way restrained by borders, God can be her own explanation. We limited, changing beings cannot be our own explanation. We need parents who supplied our genetic material, and before them apes that became protohuman beings, and before them all the earlier evolutionary story, and in the beginning the big bang or some better start. As nothing specific yet the fullest reality, indeed the ultimate source of all realities, God can just be, and his being nothing can be the other side of his just being.

LORD

The impersonal images that we use for God, need for God, are extremely valuable because as soon as we begin to picture God we fear instinctively that we shall create God in our own likeness. God will be just a great Father figure or Mother figure. We will just extrapolate God from the sun and high heaven or from the earth and primal fertility. In the worst case, we shall find ourselves addressing an old man with a long beard or fleeing a devouring maw like that of Kali, the Indian goddess who personifies time. These will be vivid images, and the more we know about the history of religious iconography the more we shall respect them, but we shall not be able to use them in good conscience without a counterbalance from impersonal images, because we know instinctively that they are limited and so not enough to render "God" safely.

Having said this, we can note the great influence that limited personal images such as "Lord" have had in the biblical religions (Judaism, Christianity, and Islam). Based on human experience of a king or ruler, this name for God has emphasized his controlling the world. It has led to a picture of God as a powerful male, the head of a state and army. One might extend the picture so that it covered "lady" or "queen," a female divine ruler, but in fact "Lord" has thrived in patriarchal cultures — those where people have taken political rule by men for granted. "Lord" could be tamed, domesticated, inasmuch as the ruler was genteel, kindly as well as powerful. It could express the devotion of the disciples to their master, the affection as well as fear, obedience, and commitment. But always it has presupposed a relationship based on unequal power. The God who is Lord is the superior in power. The person who worships this God is the inferior.

If we think of God as the Creator, the source of all the beings that exist, then it makes sense to picture him as Lord. Similarly, if we think of God as the ruler of nature, the one who commands the winds, sends his rain and sun on just and unjust alike, then it also makes sense to speak of him as Lord. He is in charge, through his power and plan. He is provident, knowing what is going to happen and determining it. Finally, he is well placed to judge the creatures whose compliance with his plan is not automatic but requires their free choice.

The waves of the ocean do not come under judgment, nor do the palm trees in the tropics. The Lord does not call them to give an account. Even the horses and sharks do what they do instinctively, with no deliberating about whether they will obey God's plan. For Eastern religious schools such as Zen Buddhism, this necessity can reveal a superiority in nonhuman nature. The plants and animals cannot err morally, and physically almost always they do what they ought smoothly, gracefully, without fits and starts. Human beings can err, do err, and often we are herky, jerky, graceless.

The judgments of God bear on the gracelessness of our free moral acts. The Lord's lip does not curl when we stumble on the playground and skin our knees, but it may well curl when we puff out our bandy little chests and say, "Hell, no, I won't go!" Yes, the Lord may have a sense of humor, as the book of Jonah implies, and certainly he may prefer feisty rebels to compliant toads. But in the center of the relationship between divinity and humanity God has to want an obedient use of our freedom because the plain, unchanging fact is that we and God are not buddies. God is the maker of heaven and earth; we are but pissant ashes. In biblical terms, God is the potter and we are the pots. In imagery from Plato, God is the great puppeteer, pulling all the strings by which creation dances.

So the proper response to the Lord, for all that he has done for us, is, "Yes. I hear and I obey." It is a further question, of course, whether what I hear, the version of God's "laws" or "word" that my culture tells me is authoritative, is in fact from God, cannot in fact be disputed. When we picture the Lord as a lawgiver, we run the danger of making an idol of the Bible or the Koran or the Talmud or any other codification of God's will. We say that God has chosen to pour the divine will into given documents, but the basis for our saying this is shaky.

For example, the basis may be the picture that we find in the Bible of God giving the Law to Moses on Mount Sinai. Or it may be parallel images that we cherish establishing Jesus or Muhammad as God's spokesman. Any such image is fraught with historical, literary, psychological, and, yes, theological problems. It is easier to say that human beings are obliged to follow the will of their Creator, who made them from nothingness, than it is to say what the will of their Creator is, at least with any historical specificity.

The advantage of the personal image "Lord" is that it can help us open our spirits toward the divine mystery with a proper docility and reverence. Inasmuch as we let ourselves admire the splendid government of creation, the power and order by which nature runs, we can move ourselves away from the egocentricity that tends to make us stupid — behave as though we were the center of the universe.

We are not the center of the universe. We are but creatures of a day, paddling in a backwater of the cosmos. Ridiculously, we forget that we shall die in what is for the universe the twinkling of an eye, and that the universe will move along as serenely after we are gone as it did while we were here. If we take this manifest reality to heart and yet find that by bringing it to a personal God whom we call Lord it loses much of its coldness, we may retain a proper sense of our smallness without losing an equally proper conviction that God numbers all the hairs of our heads.

FATHER AND MOTHER

Picturing God as parental, our Father or Mother, brings a quantum leap in intimacy. If we make God the one responsible for our lives, as though he or she had begotten us in love, we can think, in great wonder, that God cares about everything that happens to us, not just the hairs of our heads. In the New Testament, Jesus speaks about God, and to God, as though God were his dad. He assumes that God loves him through and through and will always stand by him. This assumption comes into crisis when Jesus feels abandoned on the cross, but the authors of the New Testament attribute the resurrection of Jesus to the power of his Father, as though the Father worked for Jesus a great vindication of his trust.

A few texts in the Bible, for example Isaiah 49, depict God maternally, but on the whole the biblical God is a patriarch. Eastern religious cultures, both Indian and Eastern Asian, have developed a stronger iconography featuring a motherly God. The many Hindu mother goddesses coalesce in the figure of the Mahadevi, the great goddess, while the Chinese Buddhist Bodhisattva (Buddha-to-be) Kuan-yin, and her equivalents in other Eastern Asian Buddhist cultures (Kannon in Japan, Tara in Tibet), has functioned as a maternal icon for divinity.

Inasmuch as our parents represent something primordial in our psyches, as they do in the objective origins of our physical lives, we are almost bound from time to time to picture God, the comprehensive source of our being and fate, in parental terms. Still, we may feel that such a picture is too anthropomorphic — makes God too human, risks sentimentality. How can the impersonal energy exploding in the suns and stars be a kindly parent, gentle and patient with us in all our weakness, all our folly? What warrant have we, apart from a few religious texts and our own wistful thinking, for dealing with God, the constant mystery, as though we could bury ourselves in the divine bosom, consider the divine darkness a lullaby?

This is a good question, but nowhere near so hard to answer positively, so as to support treating God as our Father or Mother, as cynics may imagine. "God" is unlimited. Any image of God that makes sense of our experience or seems to reveal useful aspects of the divine mystery is legitimate. For example, throughout religious history many peoples have depicted God as a force that we ought to fear. Their experience of nature, or of human tyrants, or of what human beings require to keep them on the straight and narrow made a presentation of God as stern, demanding a strict moral accounting, seem sensible. However, if another depiction, according to which God were a kindly parent, supportive and loving, led to similarly good effects, perhaps even better ones, why would it not be sensible to employ it?

There is in "reality," in what we intuit about the objective character of the mystery holding our lives, reason to think that God is demanding. However, there is also reason to think that God is loving. The mystery that we probe, that reveals itself to us in our most significant experiences, includes a profound suggestion that we human beings thrive only through love. For instance, unless they are loved, infants do not thrive. They are not happy; they do not develop well physically; they are slow to gain weight, muscular coordination, and mental alertness. Similarly, until they find love, young adults are lonely and feel that they are not using their full capacity.

Indeed, at no stage in the human life cycle do we outgrow our need for love or our intuition that love is the greatest, the most transforming and fulfilling, of our human experiences. When we are in love we brim with creativity, whether we are twenty-four or seventy-four. When we are in love we find courage, energy, goodness that we did not know we could muster.

Parental love is a basic kind or mode. It has its temptations to selfishness, but on the whole it is purer than romantic love or friendship. The parent benefits mainly by seeing the child happy, by enabling the child to thrive. The fulfillment of the parent as parent is the prospering of the child. Yes, the parent needs to be needed, and this may offer a valid analogy to God. In creating, God may have positioned divinity to need to sponsor the thriving of creatures, even to want to be admired like the color purple. In creating, God may have chosen to comport himself, herself, like a parent.

Stereotypically, maternal love is the fiercest, the most self-sacrificing form of parental love, and the lack of a strong maternal imagery for God in the Western religions has kept Western theology from being as attractive, effective, and persuasive as it might have been. (For orthodox Christians the Virgin Mary has never been divine.) Inasmuch as a mother identifies herself completely with the welfare of her child, whom she has carried under her heart, the love of a passionate divine Mother might often break down the last barriers in our sinful hearts, convincing us once and for all that God cares for us beyond any deserts. Brushing aside even our protests of regret and unworthiness, the divine parent, whether maternal or paternal, would (on the pattern of the prodigal father in Luke 15) rush out to welcome us home, assuring us that we shall always be in God's eyes the child who captivated her heart from our first grin.

Certainly, there are serious problems latent in the imagery of a divine parent, because many people have had bad experiences with their human parents — experiences of neglect or abuse or harshness. Nonetheless, this possible problem need not invalidate the use of "Father" or "Mother" for God. It simply requires that we retain prudence and caution. The appeal that a child has to an adult, especially to its parents, offers a wonderful entry into the rich world of positive emotions that we can imagine flowing back and forth between ourselves and a good, loving divinity. The way that the child tugs at the adult's heart, indeed the apparent evolutionary cunning expressed in the child's being so helpless and appealing as to demand care, hints at what the divine heart may be like.

If it would be wrong for us to imagine a parental divine heart without employing some critical controls, lest we become hopelessly sentimental, it would be equally wrong, shortsighted, and shortchanging to veto all such imagining. We may well be the apple of God's eye, the great delight of our Father in heaven, our Mother who makes the entire earth fruitful. God may well be charmed, greatly pleased, when we hand ourselves over to the divine will in complete trust, like exhausted little children who fall sound asleep in their parent's arms.

The past few months I have sharpened this analogy by thinking of a colleague who has just had his first child. The colleague is nearing his mid-thirties. He is quite sophisticated. But the little kid charms him completely. In fact, he would not miss bathing his son at night for the publication of three prestigious articles. Something happens when the little boy laughs that delights the father down to his soul.

The miracle of birth, the utterly basic mystery of the renewal of life through the generations, the enfleshment of love, the awesome responsibility of caring for the life of a child — these profound aspects of human existence come into sharp focus. Yet mature parents are not so much daunted as bucked up, given confidence that they can handle the challenges, because of the great love they feel. The giggle of a little child makes its parent feel super — a visitor from another planet, wonder woman possessed of extraordinary powers. When the spatulate little fingers reach out for the parent's face, the disasters of the day vanish, washed away by a shower of love in her soul.

Suppose that, without infantalizing our prayer, we let ourselves approach God like little children. Suppose that, utterly simply, we exposed to God our need, our dependence, yes even our charm. We might find that God no longer seemed far away, remote, uncaring. We might think, at least for a moment, that God wanted to eat us up, protect us completely, the way we sometimes do with our children. Later, we would have to reconcile this possibility with the evils in God's world, the pains that God's children suffer everywhere, the grounds for thinking of God's neglect. But for the moment we could be utterly intimate with God, like children playing in the bath, or asking their parents to make them well by kissing their hurts, or expecting their parents to listen to their little stories of triumph and tragedy this day.

On occasion some of the saints (for example, Therese of Lisieux) have dealt with God in childlike trust like this. The core of

Jesus' relationship with God apparently was completely trusting. If we take him at his New Testament word, Jesus was convinced that if he asked God for bread, God would never give him a stone. We may think similarly of God our Mother. If we ask her for love, care, help, and she is in any way good, can she give us back indifference?

FRIEND

I made some of my best friends when I was nineteen, removed to the country and a monastic setting. We novices were idealistic. We had time to talk, leisure to think, confidence that we could trust one another. Several of us have remained close for more than thirty-five years. Even though I see them seldom, not even once a year, when we meet our affection and understanding surge forward again immediately, as though years ago we had opened a permanent channel, an IV or shunt allowing infusion of support, communication, night or day.

To picture God as a friend, one need only develop the imagery of such an experience. Make the sense of understanding and acceptance more intense. Take away the problems of miscommunication, the frictions inevitable in human interactions. Then God can become the confidant, the teammate, the admirer, the supporter, the alter ego that one glimpsed in the best moments of human friendship. Then divinity can take your side, stand by you, in fair weather or foul, with utter dependability.

A parent can become a friend, as can a lover or spouse. God can be Lord and master without ceding the possibility of more intimate, less formal relations. In the best of human friendships, a matching of minds stands out. Friends think alike sufficiently to let them regard themselves as a majority. On important matters, they do not doubt one another. Even though the rest of the world tried to laugh them to scorn, they would barely hear because they would be singing their own duet.

My wife is my best friend, and very little divides us. When several years ago serious illness put our bond under strain, we found that it was sealing itself with epoxy. There was virtually no difference of opinion, no mine or thine concerning our welfare. The future at stake was wholly ours. The pain we carried was completely common. I had the broken back but Denise had the broken heart. My stomach wretched from the Alkeran, but Denise lost more weight. At times the intensity of the sharing became comic, leading to peals of laughter. Now and then, though, our union intensified our suffering. If we had been alone, both of us might have worried less.

Just as it has not been my personal way to approach God often through images of a Mother or a Father, so I have not approached God often with images of a friend. I am not sure why, though part of the reason is probably a fear of deluding myself. It is easier, safer, exposes us less to stay minimal, rest in stoicism. If we do not let ourselves trust God much, do not hope that God will be tender toward us and shore us up, we will not be surprised when life lets us down, will not have lost a great deal.

On the other hand, perhaps stoics have already lost a great deal. Perhaps choosing to live stoically, not letting ourselves expect much from God, is already to forfeit diamonds and sapphires, times when we and God could have been close.

We can understand the biblical figure of Israel bonded to God in covenant as a form of friendship. God pledges to be with his people, walking through time alongside them. They pledge to look to God for the meaning of all their experience. Second Isaiah, the great prophet from the time of the exile, advances this imagery of the covenant considerably. God will redeem the people from their suffering, bring them back from their bitter exile. A remnant will thrive in a new, more intimate relationship with their God. God will count the sufferings of the past as full payment for the people's sins. They will face a future washed clean of sin, pure as driven snow.

Moses was a friend of God, as was Muhammad. Though both served God as his spokesman, God treated them as more than servants, showing them affection. This implied no diminishment of the divine holiness. Neither prophet ever saw God's face. But it did imply that God could love his servants, cherish his prophets, make the cause of his favorite disciples his own. When asked by the disciple for a favor, God could scarcely refuse it. The disciple had become a bosom friend. Like Abraham haggling with God for Sodom, the friend could take liberties and not be struck down. A strange, wonderful parity had grown up between the disciple and God. Completely by God's choosing and sufferance, the disciple could assume, almost presume, that God's cause and his own were one.

As I think about my work, what I want to help advance in the world and what hold back, friendship with God becomes intriguing. I should want my work to dovetail with what I take to be the cause of God, though of course not simplemindedly or fanatically. When I think of the kingdom of God, developing patiently and peacefully like leaven in a loaf, I can speak about how the divine mystery works in history, about where the best instances of "salvation" (healing human brokenness) occur.

I find nothing triumphalistic in this imagery. Rather I am drawn by its humility. The cause of my friend God tends to unfold sweetly, suavely, far below the storms on the surface. There are few swords or trumpets. I see this cause going forward in little children growing up straight, solid workers giving honest labor, sick people and the elderly taking stock of their lives bravely, trusting God to give them a good end. For all these people, I want my friend God to be friendly — identified with their good. In all their lives, I hope that the goodness of God will be manifest, the priority of God's care over what even the best of their human friends can give them will be clear, at least to people with eyes to see.

LOVER

The Song of Songs in the Bible is one of several texts in the history of the world's religions (the Hindu scriptures showing Krishna as the lover of the *gopis* — the girls herding cows — who stand for the human soul are others) that justify imagining God as our lover. As the Jewish rabbis and the Christian church fathers interpreted this text, it represents either the bond between Israel and God or the intercourse between God and the devout individual's soul. The imagery is erotic, ardent, much concerned with beauty and longing. It reminds us that beholding God is the soul's deepest desire. It says that God must be beautiful as well as powerful and good.

Traditionally, Western religion has dealt with loving God erotically as though the human partner were feminine. Israel or the individual soul has been considered the bride or spouse of the divinity. Because in the patriarchal cultures that have prevailed in

Western history the male has been predominant, the imagery for the divine lover has made him male. His has been the initiative and control. The role of the human lover has been to wait, respond, accept what the divine lover chooses to set in motion.

Future developments of this imagery, undertaken with more awareness of the freedom human beings have to shape it, might expand the love between God and human beings in several directions. A feminine God might become the lover of a masculine human partner. Gay and lesbian possibilities might open up. However the development in fact occurs, the better theologians will strive to keep it faithful to its best potential, which is neither narrowly erotic nor antierotic. To deal well with God as our lover, the great romance of our lives, we should imagine an interaction that is both sexual and something more.

We should retain a sexual component because sex adds spice, play, and fertility. If we want God to be the delight of our lives, we have to bring into our love of God the sources of delight in our best human interactions. These include both the biological and the social bases for the pleasure, the challenge, the intrigue that moves back and forth between the sexes and keeps them willing to bear the burdens of family life generation after generation. Nowadays men and women generally do not marry and raise children only from a sense a duty. On any day, they do this best when they please one another, show one another another way to be human, a difference that never fails to be intriguing. If we imagine our relationship with God as playful, romantic, and full of delight at God's beauty, we can touch aspects of our spirits, our core selves, connected to our deepest creativity. When most creative, we want to make things of beauty, brimming with light and worth. That is what motivates large amounts of human art and science. We can want to interact with God in the same way. A strong motive in prayer can be to "seek God's face," as the Psalmist says. We can long to see the splendor of God, in either nature or the world of ideas. More tenderly, we can long to embrace God and lose ourselves in God's answering embrace. We can hope to become with God a world unto ourselves, the way that lovers can for long periods or short suffice for one another completely.

Related to the image of God as our lover is that of God as more intimate to us than we are to ourselves. This is an image deriving from a picture of God as the source of our being. We exist, step forth from nothingness, because God grants us a share in the divine fullness of existence. It is not difficult to make this existential connection personal and romantic. Inasmuch as God moves in the depths of our being, in our heart of hearts, God can be the spouse of our soul, the richer and fuller half of our very selves. We can think of sharing our lives with God as though in a marriage. We can imagine the fruitfulness of our lives, the goodness and beauty that we generate, as the fertility of a marital relationship.

The Muslim mystic Rabi'a is a good example of an espoused lover of God. She came to the point where she wanted nothing for herself, only that her beloved God be pleased. Indeed, she came to feel that wanting anything from God, deriving any benefit, would lessen her love, perhaps even render it impure. The more fully she sought only to please God, and to take away nothing for herself, the better she felt.

Christian mystics such as Teresa of Ávila and John of the Cross advanced to similar positions. They thought of their best moments as ones in which they felt wedded to God, with minimal separation in identity. On the road to this consummation, they had to endure periods of what felt like cruel separation. John's descriptions of the contemplative spirit's states of darkness and loss as purifications necessary to achieve full union with God are classic clarifications of how God tends to work in the depths of holy people. Where we ordinary people do not even imagine how it might be possible to love God so fully as to find in God our complete identity, God achieves in the innermost precincts of the saint's soul a loss of everything hindering such an identification.

In thinking about God, we do best when we respect the religious tradition in which we have been raised, or with which we identity ourselves at present, without letting that tradition stifle our creativity. Ideally, therefore, we retain our freedom to picture God as infinite, or as our Lord, or as our Mother, or as our lover — whatever, at a given time, we find most attractive — without interpreting this in a heretical, exclusivist, or unbalanced fashion. Alternatively, as long as we do not use one image so exclusively that we deny any others that are legitimate, we can approach God with any venerable iconography, enjoying great freedom. So, for example, if we find our hearts enflamed by picturing God as the romantic love of our lives, the most beautiful masculinity or femininity that we can imagine, we can and should give ourselves over to this image with vigor.

If we do, we shall probably find that dealing with God as a naked, vulnerable lover does not remove the divine holiness. On the contrary, it encourages us to see how the best erotic love is not selfish, not preoccupied with pleasure, but rather focuses on the beauty of the beloved, in God's case the infinite beauty. God is the beauty of the stars, the seas, the most winning little children. God is what ultimately draws artists to paint, musicians to compose, scientists to pursue elegant explanations. We can love God with our whole minds, hearts, souls, and strengths, as the Bible urges, because God is beautiful, lovable, without limit. We can lay down our lives for our God because we can love nothing else so dearly. The possible overtones in our relationship with God are endless because ultimate, religious love is endlessly creative. Nothing is more central to the operation of our souls, closer to the fulfillment for which our hearts long, than our love for ultimate reality.

Chapter Two

Feelings about God

OVERVIEW

I have considered some of the intellectual issues that a person wanting to live with God well ought to consider — how such a person might think most profitably. In this chapter I consider some of the emotional issues — how such a person might feel most profitably. An obvious difference in the two considerations is the amount of freedom we have. Whereas we are relatively free to think about God as we wish, entertain given images, and subject them to critical evaluation, we have considerably less freedom about our feelings for God, at least until we have become quite familiar with them.

Of course, thoughts and feelings, images and emotions, do not occur in isolation from one another. Much of what we think about God relates to feelings of anger, trust, fear, or hope — feelings that we retain from childhood or that we have been told we ought to carry. Related to these feelings are the images that we have been taught we ought to apply to God. For example, we may have been taught that God is a strict judge, and so have grown up fearing God. Or we may have been taught that God loves us unconditionally, and so have grown up with a great trust. Whatever our particular biographical experience, it behooves us to recognize how we usually picture God, feel about God, estimate our own place in the total scheme of things that "God" tends to dominate.

In this chapter I examine some of the major emotions that people are likely to find when they look in their computers under "God." After considering how feeling tends to work in our most primitive sense of God, that necessary for the word to carry any significance and the feeling to be religious, I take up a series of first positive and then negative emotions. My survey cannot be exhaustive. Numerous other feelings, both positive and negative, merit study. But by the end of the survey, the reader should find the main point clarified. The main point is the great significance of the anger or trust, fear or love, coloring our relationship with God.

At this point, it may be well to note that I am assuming that you have a relationship with God. Perhaps your relationship is more latent than developed, right now barely a blip on the radar screen. Perhaps it is more something you would like to have or are quite averse to having, rather than something in place and kicking. Even if you are not sure what your relationship with God is, though, do not hang back from the issues that this chapter raises. You do yourself a considerable favor when you take stock of what is actually ruling your soul. Conversely, you do yourself considerable harm if you keep running away from the great issues of what you are working for, where you want your life to take you, how you want your children to end up.

As most theologians see it, you cannot in fact run away from God. God is as close as your prayer that those you love will be safe, or that you will do right by your friend, or that this current crisis worrying you will pass soon. God is where you head, however unawares, when you follow a surge of wonder at a beautiful fall tree, or a surge of gratitude for a good health report, or a surge of tenderness at the thought of your child, your lover, your friend. Each of the feelings that makes us human implies more than itself. Each is a first step or two toward the question of how the world as a whole hangs together, what it means that we have feelings of contentment or dissatisfaction, that today we are whistling "Dixie" whereas yesterday it was "Mood Indigo." Are we but useless passions, feelings to no end, as Jean-Paul Sartre thought? Or does our loneliness, our discouragement, our love, our joy require that we look for more, a center where we might redeem what we've had to go through?

The negative feelings that I survey are four: fear, anger, weariness, and sorrow. Obviously, these are not emotions exclusive to a relationship with God. Children can feel some or all of them in their relations with their parents, and parents can feel them toward children. Friends can feel them with friends, lovers with lovers, colleagues with colleagues. But these negative emotions also color the souls of religious people, marking how they deal with the divine mystery.

For example, more than many religious people admit, we often fear that God has abandoned us, are angry at the way our lives are going, are tired of our moral mediocrity, or are sad that so much is wrong with the world. Such emotions shade our faith, our prayer, our sense of God itself. If we are not aware of how they are working in our spirits, what accents they are injecting into our efforts to taste and see the goodness of God, we shall not be as discerning, as wise, as we might be. We shall not have the self-knowledge that we would have if we were more aware of our emotions about God, and so we shall make more mistakes, enjoy less freedom, than what we might.

The parallel holds for our positive emotions about God. We shall only gain by appreciating better the ways and means that hope, awe, love, and trust use to shape our spirits. Our prayer; our peace and joy; our relative contentment with how the world seems to be structured, history seems to be going, what we ought to do politically to make things better; what it means to be a Jew, a Christian, a Muslim, or another species of religious believer — all these matters, and more, can operate, unfold, in richer, better measure if we sharpen our awareness of our positive religious emotions.

We have positive feelings about God. That is as certain as our having negative ones. Whenever we look forward to tomorrow, take a deep breath at the beauty of the stars, let our hearts overflow in gratitude for our spouse, or abandon our lives to what will be — whenever we do any of these fairly commonplace things, feel any of these fairly ordinary emotions, we are only a step from an important positive feeling for God.

God always lodges at the base of our spirits, dwells constantly at the foundation of our minds and hearts, drawing to herself the further implications of our significant emotions. We cannot be our full, whole selves without a connection to the mystery of God, to the farther reach hinted in any being. There is a "more" implied, wanted, suspected in every significant emotion, as in every significant thought. There is no significant emotion, as no significant thought, that is not part of a field, a web, an ecological niche tied into endless other niches.

God appears in the branching of this constant, inevitable connectedness, both emotional and ideational — in the realm of feeling as well as thought. God is beyond such branching since God is the limitlessness that gives the branching its constancy and openendedness. The technical term for this being beyond is God's "transcendence." God always lives not only in our midst but also on the far side of what we feel or think, what we sense or crave, not as a tyrant or one-ups-man but as a wonderful fullness, an inexhaustible treasure trove. We have grounds for hoping that God wants to make over to us, share with us, the best treasures she has. These grounds include all the gifts coming to us through nature and all the good counsel coming to us through the saints, so they make a huge pile.

In mathematical terms, God is an asymptote — a point out near the end of the universe, the history of creation, where all the lines would converge, the entire process would reach a centering consummation. Here the point to note is that God is this asymptote in the realm of feelings as well as ideas and physical realities. God is the beyond and consummation of all our healthy cravings, the healing of all our diseased emotions, every neurosis and withdrawal and self-hatred.

RELIGIOUS EMOTION

Before we delve into negative and positive emotions, as they relate to God, it may profit us to reflect on religious emotion generally or primitively. What makes a feeling religious, one that bears on God? No doubt, opinions can vary, but I think the gist is ultimacy, unrestrictedness. At least implicitly, the emotions that bear on God reach out to the divine mystery. Their vector heads toward the limitlessness that gives the world its boundaries; they carry some indication that they want to arrive at the world's source.

From my window in Tulsa I could see the Arkansas River, wandering its way through the city. The Arkansas is not a premier waterway, but on a fine day it sparkles. Sometimes I would remember to look out and appreciate this beauty. Then, inevitably, I would gather gratitude for the pleasing prospect it opened, the contrast it gave the flat land. Later, in the evening, just before we went to bed, I might shut off the lamps and let the lights of the city twinkle around the river, the lumens of the night make the water shimmer.

When we take the pleasure that exercises such as this bring, the aesthetic delight, and let it gladden our deeper spirit, we enter the territory of religious emotion. We are pleased not just by the river but by the entire build of creation. We are happy not just that the lights of the city shimmer off these waters but that the entire earth is often beautiful, a place where we can feel grateful to dwell. Who has made the land so appealing? How does it happen that creation can be beautiful? In what direction ought we to send our gratitude, to what address mail the praise welling up in our soul?

I am a theologian, so it is easy, instinctive, for me to impose these patterns on my emotions, look for these ramifications. But the ramifications themselves are not limited to theologians. The pattern can be there in people who barely recognize two or three biblical texts. Even more than thought, emotion is democratic. Many more people feel consolation than know how to define it. Many more people fear God, and love God, than have words to name their feelings accurately. Many more people experience their spirits moving out, freeing them from the confines of their boring jobs or painful marriages, than know clearly, reflectively, that such a movement is a genuine petition of God. We live in the midst of mystery, toward the horizon of mystery, whether we realize it or not. The more deeply, richly, and yes painfully that we are human, the more profoundly mystery tends, presses, to become our milieu.

I believe that the outreach that makes our feelings religious encourages us more than discourages. My sense, both personal and scholarly, is that dealing with the mystery of creation — loving the beauty of the world, feeling grateful that one has been placed in the land, wondering at the goodness of another person, feeling that one's child is a miracle — tends to carry with it a sense of homecoming. The mystery gives us our center. It restores us to ourselves. That is why contemplating a sunrise or a gorgeous painting feels enriching. That is why we usually leave real, personal prayer feeling better than when we entered upon it.

True, there are data from the world religions that point up the fearsome side of God, as there are trying experiences of discouragement and irritation. Many religious traditions recall that the holiness of the divine mystery can terrify people. Imagine what it would be like to look into the core of an active volcano and see the face of your god contorted with rage. Imagine how the ancient Aryans felt when they watched Indra gather together his winds and clouds and lightning bolts to concoct a first-rate thunderstorm. In the lands of the midnight sun, and so six months later the all-day darkness, think how the ice and cold might become expressions of the frozen heart causing ultimate reality to be so hard on us.

God is never subject to our control. (Only "magic," in contrast to healthy religion, tries to control God.) The nuclear explosions that create the suns and the stars blow God-the-teddy-bear to smithereens. The carnage of evolution, the gore and waste, ought to keep us from sentimentalizing God. It ought to remind us why the Psalmist sang, "The beginning of wisdom is fear of the Lord." We moderns may affect to think that this Lord is passé, no one for us to fear. That is just one of the many signs of our superficiality. We die as surely as our ancestors, many of us in agony. We rape and pillage and slaughter, so evil do our hearts remain. At many spots around the globe, we force children to work twelve or fourteen hours a day and then smile for the legislators contemplating GATT. We Americans run industries along our southern border that make Nogales and Brownsville infamous for their statistics on cancer, babies born without brains, and other monstrosities.

Do we really think there can be any order in creation and no reckoning for such heinous sin? Do you really want at death to be sent to judgment clothed in a T-shirt saying, "There is no God!"? Without an acknowledgment that God is radically other, blazingly real as we can never be, our dealings with God remain fatheaded and our lives pathetic — pain without meaning, joy bound for the dumpster. Without a healthy fear of judgment we lose a tension indispensable for holiness.

If you do not fear for your soul, do not worry that all may be for nought: you are bound to strike the holy anyway. Fear of the Lord is so basic, so close to the fundamental way we have been made, that it has little in common with the novels of Stephen King, little even with our run-of-the-mill neuroses, the narcissism dominating the best-seller lists. The fear that is the beginning of wisdom is the simple recognition that we explain nothing and are not God. We depend on God completely. This is not a matter of our choice.

It is as elementary as our mortality, the surety that we die. It is as basic as the vertigo that comes when a contemplative hears the shouting of the Commodities Exchange.

Present-day American culture tries to distract us from our mortality, the vertigo of our organized greed. In the process, it tries to distract us from the fear of God that would make us wise. Fortunately, as the great philosopher of history Eric Voegelin observed, it can never succeed completely: human beings will not live by depravity alone. The very pain in life always pushes some people to reject the trash of popular culture.

In all neighborhoods people die, some of them with dignity and a smile. People die from all families, churches, places of work. We ourselves age, sicken, and learn about pain. But the fear, the sobriety, the sadness that this inculcates need not give us the willies. Usually it can open a door for which we have been looking. Often it can lead to a blessed relief. Popular culture had been suffocating us with desires — for cars, clothes, deodorants, insurance, investments, you name it. The fierce attack of the advertisers on everything transcendent, everything that might make us think deeply or feel passionately or want to clear our lives of junk, had been wounding our spirit, making us sick, giving us an ache below the reach of any Ben Gay.

The mortality, limitation, and deep reasons for sadness that prompt us to fear God are, in contrast, healing. They do not insult us as the popular advertisers do. They treat us as adults, people with brains, beings who might be involved in a splendid adventure. I like clever ads such as those with the Energizer bunny, and I like a few prime-time television shows. Part of me is quite secular, put off by the cant of the churches, their sometimes pharisaic moralizing. In this I am more postmodern than medieval. But before I go to bed I need a few moments with the river, a few medieval thoughts from *The Cloud of Unknowing*, to help me forget the dreck of the day, the great swarm of secular nonsense, pretense, spiritual stupidity. The night that I used to see embracing the Arkansas River, now see drawing a blanket over the hills of Santa Clara, is older than either geological deposit. It stirs something deep in my being, something closely connected with sleep. Following it, I can let go of all the stuff in my life — all that I can see, imagine, manipulate, become preoccupied with. I can let the myeloma, and the silence, and the fragility of all God's suffering people take me to their lesson, the bosom of their mistress, the soft strength that was old when creation began. In the night my soul can slip its moorings, move out on the tide to God's ocean. Much as I love the world, I love God's ocean more. Much as I want to feel at home in the light, in the night something more ultimate beguiles me.

FEAR

We have spent some time on fear of the Lord, but there is more to be said. God is great and we are small. God is holy and we are sinful. These elementary realities provide more than enough grounds for fearing God, being reluctant to come into God's presence. A friend who has studied the psychology of religion for many years tells me that most people fear intimacy with God. Even people who pray regularly, and have lived upright lives, report to him that often they shun apparent overtures from God, refuse to hold still and let God love them. God is a wilderness, as well as a parent and friend. The endlessness of God can make us fear that we shall fall into a bottomless pit.

When I think of my dying, I fear the pain that it may involve and the revelation before God of sins I no longer even remember. Probing this latter fear, I realize that my images of judgment before God are quite primitive. Probably I would do better to let that mystery remain completely obscure. If God should count offenses, none of us could survive. To be imperfect, sinful, is par for the human course. Yes, there are sins and sins, grievous wrongs in contrast to ordinary weaknesses. But the sharper our intuitions of what the divine holiness must be, the keener our realization that nothing human can pass muster before God. Thus the greatest saints have counted themselves the worst sinners. Glimpsing the splendor of God, they have felt completely inadequate.

We can also fear God as part of our wholesale fear of life. All human beings are vulnerable. Everywhere human existence can be dangerous. We know little about our destiny, and even the best medical science remains helpless before many diseases. If we let ourselves appreciate the distance and coldness of the stars, we can feel that the universe is completely indifferent. The religious traditions tell us that God cares about us passionately, numbering all the hairs on our heads, but this is a proposition we have to believe, often against what we are feeling. It is not apparent, obvious, either from what we observe in nature or from how we find human beings treating one another.

When we feel afraid of God, perhaps the best thing to do is to speak to divinity itself of our fears. If we are to deal with God well, developing a successful relationship, we have to open our hearts completely. On the assumption that divinity wants good relations with us, we can imagine God realizing that he frightens us and taking steps to diminish our fear. After all, when we adults deal with a little child who seems frightened, we tend instinctively to bend down so as to diminish our height. Speaking at the child's level, we try to assure it that we are friendly and mean it no harm. Is it mere sentimentality to picture God accommodating the divine awesomeness to our weakness in similar ways?

There could be no relationship of warmth and friendship between us and God if God did not accommodate herself to our weakness. If God were indifferent to our fears, we could always feel liable to terror. So I find myself noting the ways in which a patch of sunshine or a cool breeze or a moment of inner peace seems to whisper that all is well in the world, that I need not be afraid. And, similarly, I find myself taking heart from the fact that I have survived week after week through many years. If there has been so much providential care for me in the past, perhaps there will be more in the future. This does not remove all my fear, but it helps me pluck up my courage.

Regardless of how I feel, though, I cling to the example of the Psalmist and the constant counsel of the saints, trying to share my feelings with the divine mystery. God is always there, in the *more* of my life that remains unmastered. Whether dark or light, the mystery is constant. In my anxiety, my worry, my fear, I may doubt that the mystery cares about me, that anyone is listening to my outpourings. But more often than not I come away from my outpourings feeling better for having told God what has been happening with me, how my emotions have zigged and zagged. My theology says that God knows about all this whether or not I tell him, but the psychology of the relationship that religious people try to develop with God seems to require our speaking to God from the heart. God may not require this, but I may. I may have to feel that I have gotten my fear or anger or desire for God off my chest.

When I have had my say, I ought to pause and listen. God has ways of answering, ways that are usually subtle. For instance, I may remember grounds for trusting God — counterbalancing my fears with images of the Shepherd of Israel, the father of the prodigal son. I may taste again the wonder in the biblical notion that God rejoices more in the repentance of a single sinner than in the justice of ninety-nine who were never lost. Or I may simply hear God's silence — no words, something fuller and prior. Maybe there is, after my having poured out my fears, nothing better for me to do than confront the uselessness of worry — a uselessness that the silence of God can suggest eloquently. What will be will be. After I have asked God for help and done what I could, I have to let the future unfold as it will, trusting that the way it unfolds is God's doing.

I write these words prior to a visit to my oncologist. The most recent blood tests have suggested that my multiple myeloma is on the upsurge, attacking my bones again. I have been dealing with this condition for many months, but the main thing I've learned is that little is predictable. Doctors have their statistics, which of course prove out over the long haul, but they can seldom say what will happen to patient X next week. So I don't know what the ache in my left leg means now, how dangerous I ought to regard it. I remember that the ache in my right leg was worse two years ago, when the cancer ate a sizeable hole there.

It is unsettling to play host to cancer, realize that your body has turned against you and is growing aberrantly. Sometimes it can be frightening, all the more so with a cancer considered incurable, terminal from the day of diagnosis. I have found it helpful to make God the agent of my cancer — to picture the divine mystery itself working in the plasma cells of my bone marrow. Doing this removes the terrible mindlessness, the literally crazy chaos, that otherwise seems to have been unleashed there, in the midst of me.

I do not know why a good God should decide to destroy the blood and bones of his creature, any more than I know why she lets billions live in poverty. I have to wonder whether my prior assumptions about the divine goodness were not naive. But I prefer dealing with a harsh, strange intelligence to dealing with a bru-

tal mindlessness, an evolution spawned for no reason, a cloning
mechanism blithely xeroxing me to death. I fear dying, but less
when God stands with her finger on the button of the machine,
does the copying deliberately, from the foundations of the world.
Then, despite my fear, I remember the wonderful mistranslation in
Job: Though he slay me, yet will I trust him.

ANGER

Recently I gave a talk on the theology of illness. There was nothing
exceptional about it. I referred to a few recent books by articulate
patients that lay out the significance of "illness" — how it is more
than disease because it embraces what we make of our affliction,
the meaning that we find or miss. Then I set the pursuit of meaning
through illness in the context that justified the word "theology"
in my title: the ultimate mystery that we call God. Finally, I suggested what seemed to me the most important aspects of a faith,
a religious outlook, or a disposition of soul that would respond
adequately to the needs of the terminally ill. Under this final topic
I treated briefly the need for emotional honesty with God, saying
that if we bear God grievances, are angry or frustrated or afraid,
we ought to speak of these emotions frankly, to both God and our
trusted friends.

One of my trusted friends, who had come to the talk as much
to support me as to learn about the theology of illness, reported
with some amusement that my remarks about expressing our feelings frankly, coming out with any anger at God, had upset a priest
in the audience. The priest thought that such an emotion would be
unseemly — irreligious, un-Christian. My friend mentioned the example of Job, but the priest dismissed Job as a Jew (actually, there
is little indication in the text that he is an Israelite) whose "Old
Testament" attitudes would have only limited relevance for Christians. My friend and I could only shake our heads, remembering
how the church fathers had used the Septuagint (Greek translation
of the Hebrew Bible). Not only had this priest dismissed the entire
scripture that nourished Jesus; he had also raised serious questions
about the freedom, indeed the authenticity, of his own religious
faith — its theory, if not its practice.

My friend, a physician, has dealt with many sick people, noting, as any intelligent, compassionate person would, that not a few of them complicate their illness with dubious religious attitudes. Some look on their affliction as punishment by God. Others take it as a chance to do penance. A third group find it bringing their faith into crisis: for the first time they are suffering and so can understand that the goodness of God is not simple. Throughout this complication of both their feelings and their faith, many religious people who are ill repress their actual emotions. Actually they are furious with God, deeply hurt and afraid. But they cannot face this actuality, this de facto state of their soul, because it jars violently with the image they have of themselves as religious — pious before God. So they mouth consecrated phrases, or they retreat from the whole matter of what their illness ultimately means. Sadly, inasmuch as they are divided, conflicted psychologically, they can heal more slowly than they might, or die with less peace.

I believe that we compliment God by speaking with him utterly honestly. Later I shall lay great stress on a radical honesty before God, but here let me simply assume it. If we are angry with God because something significant in our lives is awry and we are suffering, we cannot hide it from her, and we should not try. Just as it is healthier to bring feelings of fear to God than to try to suppress them, so it is healthier to bring feelings of anger. God praises Job for his honesty and rejects the pious mouthings of Job's friends. Job is speaking from the heart, laying out the legal case that he feels his grievances make. God ultimately questions this case, and Job's standing to sue, but Job's honesty God praises. He can do something with Job. Job has paid him the compliment of engaging him, holding him to account, asking him, indeed forcing him (as much as a human being can), to be God: just, reasonable, good.

How is a person who loses a child supposed to feel? Is she, or he, supposed simply to nod to God, accept God's disposition of both the child's and the parent's life, and carry on stoically with a stiff upper lip? Nicholas Wolterstorff's *Lament for a Son* shows a far more faithful way. When his son died climbing a mountain in Austria, Wolterstorff was weighed down by an agony that seemed to have no limit. It seized his soul, plunged him into darkness, and for some time he thought he might never recover. Intuitively he realized that he had to go along with this agony, let it carry him down what underground rivers it would. He could neither deny it nor stand against it. It was too powerful for him, too completely the preoccupation of his inmost self.

And he also knew that he had to share this agony with God. He could not pretend that nothing had changed in his relationship with God. His life had turned upside down. The fire at his hearth had burned down to ashes. It would have mocked God, insulted God, been supremely dishonest for him to deal with God, pray or worship, through any other lens. Like Job, Wolterstorff finally found that dealing with God on point, trying to be completely honest, forced him to broaden his conceptions. But he could not, and would not, let go prematurely of his incomprehension, his sorrow, his anger. He had to deal with God in depth, letting God be the sovereign mystery responsible for the entire build of the world, holding God to account for his son's death.

For people in significant trouble, no God of the Deists suffices. No God who supposedly made the world and then let it go its way, evolve as it would, either keeps the respect of the mature or becomes the love of their life. If we have a friend who wants no part of our hard times, the rains and storms and floods, we say that that person is a "fair-weather friend," and our saying that is not a compliment. We write that person off, as no one on whom we can rely in heavy weather. He or she just does not care enough, is not in for the long haul. When the going gets tough, we expect to see that friend pulling out of the parking lot.

Similarly, when we marry with hope and passion, we take seriously the words, "for better or worse, for richer or poorer, in sickness and health, until death do us part." Indeed, if we are religious, we may add a silent coda: "beyond death, for God's eternity." We do not cordon off the hard times, the bad patches, and define them out of the marriage. We expect to discuss, share, suffer through together what most gives us pain. So too with our covenant, our marriage, with God. The realer it is, the more passionate and absorbing, the angrier, the richer in laughter, and the more inclined to lamentation it will be. People who do not keen before God when their hearts ache have miles to go before they sleep in religious cots. People who do not deal with God in full nakedness and intimacy have yet to know God as their terrible lover.

WEARINESS

Readers who rummage in monastic literature are bound to come across discussions of acedia. Acedia is a weariness of soul, a discouragement, a sadness, an inability to muster any energy or enthusiasm or hope. It is "the noonday devil," likely to come when one has been working hard for some hours. It is the vice or temptation of middle age, a spiritual menopause. But it is not limited to the middle-aged, and it need not afflict us only in pure form, full-strain virulence like the Hong Kong flu. It can weave its way through lesser debilities of soul, making us think our feet are nailed to the floor, our mother gave birth in army boots.

Often our struggles in the world, and our struggles with God, leave us weary. It takes all our strength just to cope: keep going, hold our heads above water. If we don't have financial problems, we have kids who keep careening off course. If the kids and the bank account are fine, we have spotty health or noxious partners at work or deep discouragement at the ways of the world. We can feel ground down by loneliness, by the bickering in our religious community, or by the mediocrity in our own souls. The inertia of human maturation runs in the direction of weariness. The line of entropy tends to leave the middle-aged with less energy, more morale problems, than the young. Life gives most people a thorough trashing. It is hard to reach sixty with all your illusions intact.

What ought we to do religiously with our emotional weariness? How ought it to factor into our dealings with God? I believe that we ought to expose it to God, make it a focal point for our engagements with the divine mystery. If I am truly weary, down to my bones, my whole being is influenced. We depend on an animal vitality to give us zip, sparkle, zest. When weariness takes away this animal vitality, life is a drag, spiritual life as well as physical. We may sit or kneel in church, but we wonder why. We may take pleasure in a crisp fall day, but not as we did when we were in love fifteen years ago. Then all the leaves seemed glorious, a Heraclitean fire. Now they are nice, pretty, but they do not stir us to wonder, their reds and yellows are not miracles.

One remedy for this weariness is letting go. We can give up some of our ambitions and find ourselves the lighter for it. We can accept the fact that the fall of fifty-year-olds is not likely to be that of twenty-five-year-olds, without presuming to say what the fall of seventy-five-year-olds will be. We can even give up some of our ambitions or strong desire concerning our own health. The heart problem that has been diagnosed, the diabetes, or the cancer realistically means curtailing some activities, budgeting in more relaxation and rest. Perhaps it is time to withdraw from some commitments. Perhaps we need no longer go to convention X or on business trip Y or to vacationland Z, as has become our wont the past ten years.

The geography of our melancholy crosses the border between weariness and sadness, but in either country it takes a serious toll on the soul. Physical bases in illness are important but so are attitudes, expectations, hopes. If the onset of aging, its undeniable imprint in our skin and lungs and memories, finds us lamenting the loss of youth, we have work to do on our spirits, minds, hearts, and prayer. We ought to be defining ourselves, our core humanity, in terms of wisdom, creativity, contributions to the common good, appreciations of the splendor of the universe and the universe's God. Our test ought to be a whole love of God and a love of neighbor like our love of self.

These loves are more significant than our blood pressure or pulse or the rate at which we can jog around the quarter-mile track. A kangaroo can bounce around the track much faster, perhaps even a rhino when it's got the wind up. A human being is the only animal who can contemplate evil, have an opinion on tomato aspic, follow the accusations of Psalm 51 home to roost in personal conscience. A human being ought to grow quieter, deeper, year by year, as further experience rounds out the human comedy, tragedy, and obscurity. Often it helps me, when I am weary, to hug my weariness to me like a shawl. Softened by many tearful washings, it lies welcoming on my cheek. More and more I appreciate its warmth.

People who never get weary are probably superficial, running more on high octane than insight or virtue. People who meet the world with few illusions, blink away as little as possible, are bound to have bad days when the garbage stinks. There is a lot of garbage. Like power it corrupts, tending toward some absolute rottenness. If you say it is not garbage, rather recyclable industrial packing or next year's perfume, you are probably an idiot and not very honest. You may even love the advertising that flourishes in prime time.

I believe that human experience warrants a hopeful view of our nature, but not one that is antiseptic or naive. I believe that human beings do immense amounts of evil, cause huge quanta of pain, sometimes inadvertently, largely from stupidity, but other times deliberately, very much awares. This is a primitive wonder, a horrible surd, something only the bent find exciting. But it is also a reality, challenging us four square, and a potent source of weariness. Human beings often do not do the good that they should, and they do indeed do great amounts of evil that they should not. We are human beings, and we behave this way too, wearying others and ourselves with our sins. We can hand much of this weariness over to God, letting God take up the burden of it, by confessing our sins and asking forgiveness. But the human condition itself is no dancing party of fairy folk. The human condition is hard, demanding, more likely than not to break us.

SORROW

It is raining. A little girl stands at the window, six years old. She is a towhead, with a spray of freckles across her button nose. "What are you doing, Allie?" her mother asks. "I'm just being sad, mommy," she says. "Just being sad with the rain."

Any of us can be sad; all of us are virtually sure to be sometime. As life, standard human experience, gives us many grounds to feel weary, so it gives us many grounds to feel sad. Feeling sad, sorrowing, lamenting, is an honorable mode for religious people. It runs the danger of narcissism, self-absorption, prayer in the diction of poor-little-me, but it need not, and even when it does, who is to say that it cannot provide an honest beginning, a place to dig in and begin to grow?

If by sorrowing before God we expose ourselves to God, opening our hearts wide, then we set in motion the correction of any narcissism that sadness may encourage. For our own good God cannot indulge our immaturities, will not sanction our neuroses or refusal to grow. Allie at the window may be older, more mature, than many a coldhearted congregant in our synagogue or church. Allie at the window, responding to the rain, naming her mood, knowing what she is up to has more than her freckles to commend her.

In the writings of many mystics, sorrow, like other moods, becomes a medium or pathway to God. The holier the writer, the more the accent falls on regret that the goodness of God does not dominate the affairs of human beings as it ought. One sees in the Koran, for example, Muhammad's extraordinary sensitivity to the power of God in creation, and his parallel regret that all peoples do not bow low in homage, their tongues given over to praise. Similarly, one finds in the writings of the medieval Christian mystic Julian of Norwich a great conviction that all manner of thing will be well, but also a parallel regret that the sufferings of Christ often go unappreciated. Theologians can debate whether God suffers. There is no debating that sorrow at human beings' denial of God, or at our ingratitude for the gifts of God, occurs regularly in the most estimable religious literature. There is no denying that when we deal with holy people we find them sad that God does not rule in people's hearts (for those people's great comfort) the way that God rules in heaven.

Our human ability to measure the distance between what ought to be and what is ensures that we shall often feel sad. If we know that little children should not suffer leukemia, we are bound to be saddened by the news that Terry X is in the hospital for a bone marrow transplant. The parallel with crimes against children, and against the elderly, and against women is only too easy to make. The more concretely we know victims of such crimes, the sadder we are likely to feel. The more acutely the mismatch between what ought to be and what is presses into our flesh or psyche, the deeper our call into sadness.

But is it not illusory, some fallacy of misplaced concreteness, to think in terms of what "ought" to be? Doesn't hardheaded realism require that we bracket all such speculation and attend simply to the facts, to what actually is? Who is to say that little children ought not to come down with leukemia? What romantic reading of nature or evolution justifies such a sentiment? Do not people only increase their frustrations by maundering on about what ought to be, what would be an ideal world order?

No. It is human to wonder about what ought to be and feel sad at sickness, crime, and other sources of pain that often seem unnecessary. It is as human to wonder about these things, be moved by them, and draw from such being moved a desire to lessen human pain as it is to attend hardheadedly to the facts and deal with them realistically.

The people we ought to consider most "human," those who possess the richest blend of the most desirable qualities in either a woman or a man, are those who can long for a better world, reach out toward something utopian, without losing their footing. We ought not to want people to run away from the facts, how things actually are on the cancer wards or in the neighborhoods riddled by crime. Equally, we ought to want people to recoil from the sufferings created by how things are in such places, because without such a recoil people will not try to make things better — improve medical treatment on the wards, reduce the amount of crime.

Sadness, then, can be salutary, producing states of soul that God must find good. When we are heavy of heart because we are dealing with things opposed to how we imagine a good God wants the world to run, we are only a half-turn away from dealing with God herself. The other side of the coin, the next emotional step latent in sadness, is asking God to change the undesirable situation, making God aware of the pain with which we are having to contend.

In a word, sadness can lead on to prayer — intimate sharing of what we are feeling with God. Fairly easily we can move from the blue or bleak feeling dominating our hearts to crying before God, letting our tears flow freely. There is a gift of tears, reported by many saints. It is useful, a great help to melting hard hearts. It is not self-centered, but it is deeply emotional.

When we cry because of the sadness in our hearts, we feel the need of God, even the hope that God will be moved to help us. We feel the misery of the so many of God's creatures who are suffering, and for the moment their misery is our own — the borders melt away. So we can pray: God, give us the gift of tears. Help us to admit our sadness. Let us feel bad at the great suffering of the world, the pain and frustration in so many places, and do what we can to lessen it. Do not let us close our hearts, become hard to reduce the impact. Take us to your own heart, whatever sorrow you yourself feel, that we may understand better how you yourself cope.

HOPE

Human moods are notoriously changeable. People who give themselves over to their feelings without any critical control can move
this way and that like a weather vane. But as long as we keep a
portion of our spirit detached, aware of what is happening, we
only profit from entering our moods generously, not running away
but moving with them. So, for example, if we move into sadness
we can see how it need not end at a blank wall. It may sometimes
angle around a corner into hope.

Hope is the unexpected opening in the wall, the ray of sunshine
that comes out of the dark cloud and reminds us that only rarely
does it rain all day. Hope is also the squiggling of the human spirit
that occurs frequently in Seattle or Portland to find ways of enjoying the rain, calling in the Irishisms and speaking of "soft days."
There are lovely shades of gray. There are captivating times when
the rain moves across the bay toward us, like nature's free wash.
All that hope needs to function and help us is a little creativity, a
way of poking its head out of the battened hatch and sniffing the
breeze.

Though I have terminal cancer, I can still register a brilliant
sunrise, a quick dash of wit from a friend, the great legs on the
brunette in the brown tights and short skirt. Though I have to start
a new round of chemotherapy in the afternoon there is time for a
nice lunch, and I would be perverse not to take it, enjoy it, roll it
around my tongue and let it gladden my spirit. When I have a will
to discover beauty in the world, things to celebrate, I am apt to
find them. When I fight my temptations to depression, I feel more
like a man.

I am not saying that hope should be fatuous or foolish. I like the
distinction that many authors make between optimism and hope.
The optimist says that things are sure to get better. The hopeful
person says that things may get better and that the future has
more possibilities than we can know. Optimism suggests a view
of God that I do not find the facts, the empirical data, to warrant.
Hope suggests a view of God that the Bible, the reports of religious people the world over, and my own experience justify. I do
God a disservice when I hunker down in my woe and refuse to
keep hoping that tomorrow will bring good news. I also do God

a disservice when I fudge the facts, turn a blind eye to the horrible heaps of suffering in the world, and play Pollyanna, Mary Poppins, Joe the Bagel.

I need hope to deal well with God, and dealing with God at all honestly tends to increase my hope. I need hope, for example, to pray well because I have to come to God humbly, not as a know-it-all. God is God — completely different from me. In my imagery, my theology, God knows and I do not. God has the power to make significant changes in the world, in peoples' bodies and minds and hearts. My power is limited. So it seems good for me, profitable and healthy, to focus on God rather than myself. It seems realistic, the right orientation, to get out of my limited self and concentrate on the limitless divine mystery, the wonders that God may work.

Doing that, I soon realize again that I cannot tie God's hands, presume to say what God can and cannot do. I do not expect God to cure my incurable cancer, but I cannot say that God cannot. I do not see what purposes moved God to allow cancer, any more than warfare and rape, but I have to say that God can have purposes beyond my ken, ways of knitting evils into the fabric of history that may, from some wider or higher perspective, bring out a more beautiful pattern.

Hope is a marvelous quality, very congenial to religious, truly holy people. In Christian tradition it has often been called one of the "theological virtues," a power or capacity accompanying sustained dealings with God and reception of God's "grace" (help, favor, life). Some of these implications are simple to recognize. For example, virtually everyone finds that dealing with dour, negative people soon becomes trying. Such people expect nothing good to happen. Their instinctive reaction to any new proposal is to reject it: it is not likely to do much good, bring about much positive change. And so they throw water on the ideas of others, dampening their enthusiasms. A little bit of such people goes a long way. The small value in their caution, their reminding us not to be naive, quickly gives way to their becoming a burden and our wishing they would take their hopelessness elsewhere.

I repeat that the hopeful are not simpleminded optimists. But they are people who keep the future open. They do accent the positive, pay more attention to the good possibilities than the bad. And, if we are wise, we cherish them for this. We recognize how much we depend on their good cheer, their courage, their willingness once again to give "it" a try, give us a hearing. In our families, our places of work, our religious communities, our civic activities — in all the places where we are trying to get things done, make improvements, and clean up messes — we need people, allies, who are hopeful.

So too in our own souls. We need friends and selves and a God who are hopeful. If our ways of thinking about God are not hopeful, we shall not pray with zest, feel encouraged to serve the poor, look upon the natural world, the network of ecological niches, as footprints of God. If we imagine God to be looking over our shoulder like a prune-faced schoolmaster, poised to pounce on our every mistake and criticize us, we shall not take the moral risks we ought, never catch a glimpse, get a clue, of what Martin Luther saw when he urged his followers to "sin bravely."

God is not a moralist, let alone a prude or a prig. God laughs at most of our follies, and in God's eyes sex is not the first or most important moral matter, nor is bad language. Hardness of heart is far more important. Anyway, God is less concerned with our sins than with our prospering, our joy. When the New Testament pictures the messianic banquet, it imagines feasting — eating, drinking, making merry. Its God likes wine, women, song, and its God weeps when his people are not happy, have to trudge along in want or misery. So the authentic God, in my opinion, encourages us to hope — for good times in this life and after this life for eternal fulfillment, times consummately good.

AWE

Nowadays it can seem that awe is an emotion, a religious passion, from a bygone era, when human beings met the physical world with far fewer defenses and far less technological power. Florinda Donner, an anthropologist gone native in South America among the Yanomami, expresses this emotion well: "An overwhelming sense of awe brought me to my feet as the sky in the east flowed red and purple along the horizon. The clouds, obedient to the wind, opened to let the rising disk through. Pink mist rolled over the treetops, touching up shadows with deep blue, spreading green and yellow all over the sky until it changed into a transparent blue" (*Shabono* [New York: Delacorte, 1982], 163–64). The world can be so beautiful, so preternaturally splendid, that it brings the soul to its ground in awe, precipitating a mute worship.

Physical scientists occasionally experience a cognate awe, when the proportions of the natural world crash in on them. Staggered by the reach of the nebulae, the intricacy of the immune system, or the complexity of a single acre of marshland, a scientist can let the jolt of such knowledge travel down the sinews of the spirit into the nerve endings of the inmost self, where something electric can occur. The mouth of the mind falls open. A primal stupidity moves in like fog. There is nothing to say, nothing definite to feel. It is clear that all mortal spirit ought to remain silent, ought simply to adore the mystery overwhelming it.

Awe always opens the soul directly to God. No lesser object solicits the real thing. In awe the creature rubs the raw edge where its being comes into it from what is not created, what is simply, without condition or limit or derivation. Looking up at the rock face of El Capitan in Yosemite, I have felt this emotion start to build. El Capitan is just there, thrown into being in this stupefying fashion, and its being there points beyond itself, to the mystery that anything is, that so many things step forth from the void, and that we human beings have minds that can contemplate this wonder, warm to it in love.

In the context of worship, which is always summoned by awe, the human being tends to prostrate itself before the holiness that it senses in the divine mystery. The emotion is complex, including fear, joy, an outburst of energy-to-praise, and an awareness of power. The holy is the real, in stark contrast to the derivative and changing. The holy burns in the intensity of its unique reality, assuring that the soul will parse it as fire. It burns up the unreality of all other things, the beholding self included. In the intensity of truly passionate, fierce worship, the self disappears. There is only the divine mystery, glowing like cobalt, an ingot of a metal never seen elsewhere. The human self cannot come near the holy and live. The sheer reality, the blazing isness of the divine, would blast the unreality, the limit and contingency, of the human self to smithereens. So the awed self cowers as before an atom smasher, afraid it will be pounded back to primordial dust, mesons of nothingness. Unless God beckons it gently, with outstretched hand, it will never know joy.

Though it is rare today for us to sense these emotions, dwell in awe of any scope or heft, we cannot deal with God well without feeling the back of our necks tingle now and then, as the fear and fascination of God lay light hands on our souls. The absence of God, the apparent silence and nothingness, seduce us into thinking that the mystery has no power, does not care. Well, maybe this is not the case. At the least, whether the mystery exerts itself, comes into our lives with a thump, is up to it. The final say will never be ours. God can raise up children of faith from inert stones. God is God. That God is God, and only God, is the seed of awe — the ovum, the zygote if we wish.

Should God give you any stirring of awe, any conception, tend it like the best of mothers, the most grateful of those made fertile. In you has come to dwell, for a moment but maybe more, a sense of what cannot be sensed, a first stroke of a beginning letter of the word spoken in all the stellar explosions. These images are worse than inadequate, but so are all others. The awe in your soul is not for burning or doing or chanting. It is just for being — letting God be in you and through you, for holding still and trying to abide.

Sometimes, in the thick quiet, when my writer's corner becomes the mouth of a cave, I find abiding like this consoling, as though for a moment all things were well. God is the being of my being. The opacity in which I wait is dumb but not stupid. What separates things is what is unclear. Their unity in God is obvious. These moments move along. It is laughable to think that I might control them. But when they return I recognize them. Abiding shows a gracious sameness, a common incline down which the soul rolls toward the depths of awe.

LOVE

We can love the mystery of the abiding of God's being, and it feels wonderful to do so. Any love, in fact, opens a door toward the love of God, the appreciation that the divine mystery is awesomely good. What distinguishes the love of God from our other kinds is its unrestriction. The desire and appreciation that move out toward God find no place at which to stop. When they do stop and rest, it is not at a place. It is on an ocean or in a cloud or beyond all imagery or thought. Usually we love in the train of thought, in pursuit of something that has struck us as beautiful or good. But with God the thought, the understanding that we gain, often comes after the love, in the love's train.

What do we learn from loving God? What crumbs feed our minds? That we should abide — hang on, in the center of our being, and prefer simplicity to complication. In love our being coincides with that of God. We feel that God is in us, at our core, along our foundation. The more fully we enter into ourselves, finding our core, the more fully we enter upon God. God is more ourselves than we are. The bases for a full pantheism (thinking that we are God literally or that God is the sum of all beings) are slight. Our mortality, ignorance, and sin are far too great to allow us to make this mistake. But God is more what we are, who we are, our particular being, than we are. God has more claim to our name. We are not likely to make this partial pantheism (sometimes called "panentheism" — God *is* in creatures and creatures are in God) compelling to many outsiders, but the more simply we pray our way to the depths of our being the less we ourselves can doubt it.

We love God for the good things we see around us, the good things that happen to us, and we struggle to hang on to our love when bad things rise up, proliferate, slash our bodies, our minds, whole classes of downtrodden peoples. As we wrestle with the plain facts, the central pattern of virtually every human story, we realize that we do not understand God at all. So we can worry that our love was only for an idea that we have outgrown or for an adolescent sweetness. Looking at the wreckage of our faith that trouble threatens, we can wish that God would leave us alone, let all the lights stay out, permit us to stop loving the divine mystery, let us lick our wounds in an easier agnosticism.

But God will not leave us alone, any more than God will put all the lights on and drive away the darkness of our human condition. Almost always, God insists that we live in twilight, shadow, a world where the colors keep changing. If God ever puts on all the lights, it is on the far side of our deaths. Realistically, maturely, until death we have to expect to grapple with God, wrestle like Jacob. God will bless us, but we shall limp, battered by clubs from the dark.

I am not sure how best to prepare children for this near-certainty. I do not think that God is cruel, but I shake my head at what any child may have to go through before it reaches its final destiny. Still, obviously, I have little say about how God will deal with any child, any adult, no matter how close to me. God is more intimate to them than I can ever be, as God is more intimate to me. The love of God is more the central drama in their lives than any love of mine can ever be. God is for all of us the single overwhelming passion. For all of us the remarkable dictum of Karl Rahner holds true: the greater our union with God, the more freedom we have, and the more we develop our true selfhood.

It does not matter finally whether or not we appreciate this being joined to God as to a Siamese twin. We do not have to like it or agree to it consciously, generously, piously. It simply happens because we are simply human. If any light rises in our minds, we know at least flickers, beginnings, of the understanding of God. If any want beyond the purely physical shapes our souls, a passion for God is stirring. Breathed there ever a soul so dead that it knew no mental light, no passion for what ought to be? At the beginning of *Faust* Goethe speaks for us all: What does it mean that I am so sad? It means that I am made for what is more, better, other than what I meet in everyday life, in the mirror morning after morning. It means that to be human is to be dissatisfied, driven out of the world, allowed here, in space and time, no comfortable home. The true habitat for humanity is heaven. Before heaven, all shoes pinch, no chair is fully comfortable. How can you know when you are in love with God, hungry for God, mooning or suffering or touched? When your passion has no precise focus, is not being in love with X or Y, not even being in love with love. Certainly, a woman or a man can stimulate it, as can a lemon moon or a painting of genius. But none of these can explain it or satisfy it. It is not satiable, for it moves far below lust or greed, matching up with the unrestriction of your human soul, the spark in your clod.

Your love of God is the being of your being, your quintessential self, set in its characteristic action, which is passion — suffering, active waiting, what the philosophical Taoists called *wu-wei*. You want everything, but in peace. Nothing you can see or feel or think meets your want, which is your self thrown out to the farthest stars, cast down to the ocean floor. You are not in love as you recognize from any other experience. You do not know where to give yourself, to whom to turn, what you ought to pursue. You only know that you are not going to be satisfied. The measure of your soul, the ratio that your deeper mind seeks, is a line moving you out of the world. It is an unseen measure, an unmoved mover. It is the lure of your spirit, the final cause.

When this final cause has gotten its hooks into you, your ordinary life is ruined. Ever after you know that you cannot make do with money and banking, productivity and pleasure. The Freudian "love and work" is on the right track, but it still misses the mark, having no prayer, because no God. You need to love unrestrictedly, which means to pray — seek God, wait upon God, rivet your soul to the divine mystery — more and more constantly. You need to labor for the fruit that endures, the foretaste of the garden of paradise.

Naturally, sometimes you are more confident about the reality, the revelatory value, of these feelings. In bad times they can appear to be the cruelest of illusions. Finally, however, you should realize that you have to choose what times you are going to consider crucial. What is going to be the most significant of your experiences, the Archimedian lever, the canon within the canon? No one else can make your choice for you. It has to fit just your conscience, just your life. The love you bring to God is a gift no one else can duplicate. You have to decide what it shall be.

TRUST

The last of the feelings about God that I treat is trust. If we are right to express our fear of God, our anger, our weariness and sorrow, our hope, our awe, and our love, so we are right to express our trust. Trust is a feeling of letting go. We stop battling, fighting, resisting, insisting on our own way — in part because we are weary, but in more important part because we have sensed the trustworthiness of God, the rightness of handing ourselves over to the divine mystery. So we open our hands and let our lives, indeed the whole drama of history, spill out, to be gathered up by God as God chooses.

Though older people have more grounds than younger people for seeing the inevitability, the final reasonableness, of opting to trust God, trust is not the exclusive property of the elderly. For some months I watched a fifteen-year-old girl negotiate a possible change in schools. Her parents were not completely happy with her local high school, so they had her apply to a prestigious prep school nearby. Two uncertainties dogged her application. One was whether she would be admitted. The second was whether, in the crunch, her parents would find themselves able and willing to pay the high tuition. The girl had no inordinate passion to attend the prep school, though in prospect many aspects were appealing. To get herself motivated to go through the interviews and application forms, she had to make acceptance a mark of distinction — something worth the trouble. However, the uncertainty about her parents' finances led her to detach herself from any particular outcome. She would do her best and then let be what came to be. I saw her achievement of this balanced position as a remarkable accomplishment for a fifteen-year-old — a feat that would have done a much older person proud. I also saw it as a species of religious trust. Under the psychological moves to protect herself against rejection, she seemed to look on the future as God's doing. Whatever came to be, she would put the best interpretation on it.

In the days when I was intrigued with Erik Erikson's studies of the life cycle, I pondered the foundational importance of trust. Unless infants can entrust themselves to the world — their parents, the physical milieu in which they find themselves — they cannot thrive. Unless those caring for them equip infants with a basic confidence that the world is trustworthy, the children will not explore the world as they ought and so will not grow optimally.

The paradigmatic image is the child on the verge of walking. The adult holds out her hands. The child staggers forward, chirping and gurgling. The adult has to catch the child reliably enough for the child not to fear it will get hurt. The adult also has to keep the experiment valid by letting the child fall now and then, so that the hardness of the ground, the perils of the physical world, make their proper impact.

"Realism" is a delicate compound of protecting the child while letting it learn the consequences of its actions. There is no realism if the child can never fall down and go boom. There is also no realism if the child only suffers and is never caught, protected, tossed up toward the ceiling for soaring delight.

The God we have to trust, if we are to mature religiously, is always mysterious. We never get faxes or E-mail telling us exactly where he or she will be, exactly what interest rates are now in force and how much we can borrow. Can we give our hearts over to so mysterious a deity? Can we trust the divine silence enough to love it passionately? The answer has to be yes, if any significant relationship with God is to develop, but the grounds for such a yes are far from obvious. The same God whom we bless for the beauty of the world we may curse for the pain that life can impose. The wider we open our hearts to the divine goodness, the more vulnerable we make ourselves.

Still, death ensures that the odds stack themselves in favor of trust. If we are to make our peace with death, we have to find a way to accept it, ideally a way that lets us call it good. The most direct way to do this is to let death epitomize the demand for trust that the divine mystery is always raising in our spirits. Inasmuch as our certain dying solicits our reconciling ourselves to living at the behest of another, every time that we come to grips with human mortality we hear a call to let ourselves go, entrust our fate to something larger than our own vision or comprehension.

We may do this impersonally, simply slipping into the flow of all animal existence, merely moving alongside the elephants and tigers and butterflies. Or we may do it personally, making our deaths an intimate affair between the divine mystery and ourselves. Following the second, personal model, trust becomes familiar: the emotion we have known since we were toddlers, the coin of the realm of friendship. God is our parent, our friend, one who solicits our trust, who promises to be trustworthy. God is bound to us by the covenants, trustworthiness, and solemn promises that express what the Hebrew Bible means by *hesed:* steadfast love. We have known God, entrusted ourselves to God, since our youth, when first our lives began to take shape. We had to plunge in: choose a college, say yes to a romance, take a job. All this requires us to trust that things could turn out well. We are not dealing with a stranger at the bottom of this plunging in, though we are dealing with a mystery. Over time the mystery to whom we entrust our-

selves can become familiar — the same darkness or silence, barren
or pregnant, with which we have dealt often in the past.

When we think about God personally, trust takes on interesting, perhaps even crucial, angles. If God has a personal concern
for us, the particular providence that John Henry Newman loved,
then our trusting God becomes dramatic. God has to wait on our
responses, to see whether we shall agree to the plan he wants to
unfold. A motherly God has to bide her time, looking for the right
moment, the one when we may be able to understand why a certain demand is bearable, perhaps even necessary. Trust fits well the
model of religious development according to which God expects
us to proceed by trial and error. God trusts that we will be good
enough at heart, sufficiently honest and loving (by God's own sufficient grace), not to make a hash of our freedom. We trust that
God does leave us free, is not a narrow moralist, understands our
need for experiment, failure, even sin.

So it goes, in a truly interpersonal, dialogical relationship with
God. So it goes when our feelings can be honest, spontaneous, genuine. We can trust God enough to come home dirty and defeated,
a failure in our own minds. We can believe that God would rather
have us come home to lick our wounds than stay out in the cold,
ashamed not to be immaculate. Can we trust God enough to let
her see our failures, our brokenness, all the parts that are ugly?
Can we have a full, rich, truly heartwarming relationship with God
unless we do?

God waits on our trust. God hopes that, one day, we shall lower
the barriers, perhaps definitively, and accept happily what we have
become. The authors of self-help books write a lot of drivel about
accepting ourselves, but a smidgin of it is on the mark. God is
much less put off by our failures than we are. God knows the
blueprint to which we have been made, every lump of fat in our
bottoms and heads. God's care, God's stake, is less the performance than the sharing. If we are living with God, sharing both the
suffering and the shouting for joy, our performance is quite secondary. We can never please God, in the sense of bringing home a
report card that will puff God up. However, when we trust God
with our sorest feelings, our rawest pains, we can win God's heart.

Chapter Three

Working for God

OVERVIEW

I have dealt with thinking about God and some of the feelings that dealing with the divine mystery tends to entail. In this chapter I move into closer relations with God: working together, cooperation, the active influence of God in our actions and thoughts, the constant overlap of our intentions and those of our Creator. Some of this cooperation can be deliberate on our part, the efforts of religious people to orient their lives wisely, by reference to their first source and final end. Other parts are simply given, inasmuch as we experience that "God" sets the ultimate horizon against which we creatures think, beckons as the full treasure that alone can satisfy our needy hearts.

I begin by noting the natural inclination of many human beings, perhaps of human nature itself, to seek God: search for a complete satisfaction, something more lasting and total than what mortal life seems to allow. People who follow their eros, their ardent desire, for a beauty that does not tarnish, a justice that does not tilt, are likely to move out of ordinary human existence, realizing that they are reaching for "heaven." If they deal with this fact, this actual movement of their minds and hearts, properly symbolically, they can learn a great deal about their own makeup.

We human beings do not know what we want, cannot produce any photograph or exact blueprint, but we can sense that "we have here no lasting city," that the spiritual substance lying under our sensation, our imagination, even our simplest thoughts reaches out for a whole, an infinity, bound to defeat our efforts to control it but also able to nourish us as nothing material or partial can. John of the Cross is famous for this theme, but it is a commonplace among people drawn into regular dealings with God. When they obey the Psalmist's injunction to seek God's face, they intuit that they may end up alongside Moses, trying to find a way to abide close to one whom, in fact, they cannot see directly and still live.

The physical analogy for this intuition, clearer to us than to the generation of Moses, is the explosion of thermonuclear energy. The being of God that makes the world has to include, in part express itself through, the creation of suns and stars. Certainly, the biblical authors want to place the Mosaic God, the Lord of the covenant given on Mount Sinai, at some distance from the raw deities of natural power, storm and fertility, that their pagan neighbors worshiped. Thus Elijah did not find his Lord in the storm but in the still small voice of the aftermath. Nonetheless, when we deal with God, the full significance of the limitlessness of the sole ultimate source of "reality," of all that stands out from nothingness, can finally make its impact. Literally, we are beyond our depth, out of our minds and hearts, seeking and perhaps being sought by we know not what, by a reality too primordial and complete for us to name it, grasp it, exert any significant control over it. All control and priority belong to it. It makes the sun to rise, the rain to fall, and we obviously do not. Yet we can find our lives taking shape as journeys into this known unknown. We can realize, with amusement as well as startlement, that we are constructing a map of our time that is taking us toward a *terra incognita*. The land is unknown because it is unknowable on ordinary terms. The face that we seek has no planes that hint at its dimensions.

My second consideration in this chapter is receiving God. If seeking God implies that the dynamics of human action tend to move our minds and hearts out of narrow confines, limited space and time, then receiving God implies that God on occasion reaches into our normal sphere of space and time, to help our outgoing along. Now and then a breeze stirs in our spirits, arising we know not how, that takes us toward the Golden Gate, out of the city, up-country, where the wine grows. Or we wake with our depressing problem solved, a gift from the therapies of our dreams, and so the new day stretches forth like one of the six of the biblical account of creation. We know in our bones that we have a chance to make a difference, accomplish something of which we can be proud. The natural world lies ready to hand, not to be exploited but to be nurtured, brought along. The colleagues with whom we had been uneasy seem more tractable because we ourselves are at peace. For the moment, grace has anointed our awkwardness, and so we have sensed how human relations might flow in heaven, what a properly playful or lightly ritualistic common existence might be.

Third, what ought we to say about serving God? If we decide that the strange love stirring in our hearts, the inarticulable intrigue that we find in dealing with the divine mystery, is becoming a regular allure, an invitation to trysts late at night, to contemplations of the sunrise, how ought we to think about making this love our mistress, the lady fair we would delight to serve? Is the proclamation of her beauty, and eventually also the delineation of her demands, a work that can take over a life properly? What does one serve, announce, sell, and try to promote when "I know not what" is the core of the message? Trying to serve the real, living, mysterious, unco-opted God is a strange, wonderful business. Whatever brings out the best in people, their most burning creativity, their least questionable desire for justice, seems a good work or influence. Whatever widens their hearts, allays their fears, decreases their anxieties, increases their generosity and compassion would seem to carry the mark of what we want "God" to do for us.

Dealing with God has to make us better, facilitate our realizing our positive potential. Otherwise, there is little sense in trying to be "religious," working to retie our lives to the divine tether. The small gods of many of the churches seem a bad bargain, compared to the breadth and width of the human spirit not forced to run on a narrow ecclesiastical gauge. The pharisaic, clerical mind gives God a bad name, while the murderous soul of the religious terrorist makes God repulsive, the outright enemy of human decency. So what God we serve, how pure a mystery, matters enormously. All religious leaders should be at pains to clarify the primacy of human conscience in these matters, and the falsity of much religious dogma. Believing that genuine religion — proper worship of the beautiful, only fully real, divine mystery — is the best of human activities, we should be hard on the corruption of religion, which has visited on history some of the worst depravities.

Fourth, we can make explicit some of the norms, criteria, and rules for discernment that holy people have developed through the centuries as they sought to purify their service of God and make sure they were not soiling their linen treasure. For example, those who persevered in dealing with God intimately tended to find their emotional satisfactions mattering less. God ought to be served for her own sake, if need be at cost. The generous knight or maid cared more for the Lady's satisfaction than any praise or reward. The Creator blazed so purely, had of himself so little to do with feeble, finite creatures, that simply acknowledging the Creator and trying to follow what seemed to be his code for the world, his plain instruction on how to live well, could become a strong passion.

Yes, dealing with God tended to legitimize an instinct that God is personal, as well as impersonal. Most of the saints have reported that treating God as trustworthy, even abandoning one's fate to God like a child crawling onto its parent's lap, brought a good spiritual result. But such saintly familiarity with God never took away the otherness of God, the need for what the Bible calls fear, the requirement that we not grow presumptuous. We only exist because of God's good pleasure, and we only prosper by God's free grace. A service of God, an engagement with God, that forgets these bedrock truths remains impure (and probably will soon get its comeuppance, if God acts characteristically, out of mercy for the weakness of the creature and the need to draw it out of its illusions).

The fifth topic — easing anxiety — helps suggest the range that defining human existence as most ultimately an interaction with divine mystery can open up. We cannot work for God, collaborate with God maturely, without easing our anxieties about living beyond what we can know with empirical certainty, living by what the world religions, in varying ways, call "faith." Worry does no good. Even fear that we are deluding ourselves runs its course, as we realize that we have no other serious choice. We have been bitten by God, and though sometimes we wonder whether the bite is from love, not from a scorpion, we go back to scratch it again and again. We can do no other than return to our post, look forward to the dawn, the great symbol of spiritual illumination, because the old life we led, down in the cellar with the barrels, holds little appeal. So our anxiety tends to run its course. If God is dead, or never was, then nothing matters ultimately, and anything is permitted. Then might makes right, and chaos is as legitimate a king as order. To work for God in peace, we have to see all this clearly and then set it aside. We ought never to deny the more-than-rational character of faith and yet also never deny the many ways in which faith is superior to reason, considerably more human.

My sixth topic, discernment, provides the chance to follow the human spirit into nicer, more delicate operations, where it waits upon God in prayer and learns how the Spirit of God, divinity considered as the personal tutor of the human spirit, tends to instruct it in matters of courtesy, etiquette, what the creature ought to do when given a work, a service, or an inspiration (a spiritual kiss). The God properly represented as liking covenants, pledging to share the fate of his creatures and walk with them through time, depends on a language of images, touches, moods. Committed workers want to master this language, let the Lord attune their ears. They want to hear the Way in the morning, get clear the marching orders, and to do this, experience shows, they have to pay attention, making sure that they have not grown narcissistic, let alone hardened their hearts (against what can be imperative claims). All this work, interest, obligation can fly under the flag of "discernment." People trying to become good religious workers, competent at whatever craft mystical love requires or fashions, realize that they need to beg from God a fine balance, a strong realism, rooted in dispassion, in freedom from untoward desire, in a genuine longing to let only the one true God rule their hearts.

Seventh, liturgy is the common prayer, the formal "work of the people," that brings many of these interests, concerns, to social focus. Gathering for their liturgies, peoples of various traditions have supported one another crucially. They have remembered their deepest convictions, both historical and theological, and in doing so they have reaffirmed the strongest roots of their community, their traditional peoplehood. The deepest center of any traditional culture is the *cultus,* the worship, that has focused the myths, rituals, symbols of ultimate meaning by which that culture has stood. Thus Muslims have been people of the Koran, formed most intimately by a demand for submission to the gracious revelation given by Allah through Muhammad. Jews have been people of Torah, finding their identity again and again through the rituals of the Sabbath, the Passover, and the other canonized remembrances of how their Lord led them out of Egypt and consecrated them on Sinai. Buddhists have been members of a *sangha,* a community of monks and laity, understanding itself through the teaching (Dharma) of Gautama, the sage who solved the problem of suffering. When they have chanted the scriptures conveying the teaching of the Buddha, Buddhists have let the sounds and images swell, making mantras and mandalas. Emerging from such ceremonies, they have felt renewed as disciples of an unfailing wisdom, beneficiaries of a message of great liberation, an invitation to an almost delicious peace and compassion.

The members of the various religious groups that have celebrated such liturgies have tended to march out of their services charged, energized, for witness, my eighth topic. They have tended to feel that the good news they have heard, the great gifts of liberation they have been offered, exist for all people, objectively, as the largess of God. And so many such believers, workers, have thought witness, testimonial, both natural and obligatory. They ought to tell others about the magnificent deeds of God, the reality of God. They ought to show in a dozen ways how those deeds enrich a life, ease suffering, raise people's sights to let them suspect that death may not be the last word, that intercourse with divinity takes the creature outside of death, onto the bosom of One fully alive, intrinsically creative. The "martyr" is the witness par excellence, giving testimony in blood, but ordinary witness is more than adequate, indeed can be preferable. Simply to do what one ought to do, carry the burdens that the given day imposes, can be the most influential witness, saying that the worker loves doing what she does because it is her Lord's will for her. The last topic that I consider in this chapter, dying, takes us to the end of the contract between the religious worker and God, where the final proportions of the collaboration come clearest. Generally we die when and as God determines, outside of our own control. There is little we can do about this, except the one thing necessary. If we accept it with grace, move with it as God seems to require, we can complete a fine career. Dying is repugnant to us, instinctively. We have an animal instinct for survival, a primitive will to live, that resists dying mightily. How the Spirit of God tames this will, without enervating us, can be intriguing. In the final section of chapter 3, we can exercise our imaginations somewhat, to picture how the Spirit tends to make dying finally look good to us, a consummation devoutly to be wished.

SEEKING GOD

A nine-year-old boy looks out the window, seeing the summer stretch before him. He is in the second week of vacation, when the pleasure of not having to pound out at 7:00 A.M. for the school bus has started to fade and he is getting bored. He has tennis lessons at noon, a soccer game on Thursdays, but there are not many kids his age in his suburban neighborhood, few suitable playmates. The boy lazes around watching TV, eating potato chips. He is too young to be a self-starter on a science project or something artistic. His summer is becoming a burden.

At this point the boy's dad makes three suggestions. First, the boy has talked about becoming a better swimmer, now that they have their own small but inviting in-ground pool. He could take a few lessons, to improve his strokes, and then begin swimming significant distances. That would get him into good shape, also present him with a regular challenge. Each day he could measure himself against what he had accomplished the day before. If on Thursday he did forty laps, whereas on Monday he had done thirty, he could feel considerable satisfaction. The father knows his son. He has smiled at the son's competitiveness. The trick would be to teach the son to compete against himself, ideally without the father revealing his amusement.

The father also knows that swimming, running, and similar other private pastimes can nourish imagination and reflection. Going up and down in the pool, his son might have submarine adventures, run silent and deep. He might win the Olympics or cross the English Channel. He might even find his way to Atlantis, imagine himself living under the sea. One of the main tasks of childhood is to develop a frisky, creative imagination. One of the main ways to avoid boredom and be productive in later years is to realize how our minds work, what the "image of God" in us means.

The father's second suggestion is that the son travel with him now and then, perhaps twice a week, when he makes calls on his customers. The kid could bring along a book, for the times when he had to stay in the car, but often he could come into the factory, get a look around. Between calls, they could talk about what the father does, the products he sells, why salesmanship fascinates him. This is all new to the boy, but the mere fact that his father is taking such an interest in him piques his curiosity. He is flattered, and he begins to look forward to going to work with his dad, learning about business.

The third suggestion that the father makes actually comes from the boy's mother. She has musical talent, and she thinks that her son may have inherited it. But she has gotten nowhere with suggestions that he study the piano. The father worries that the son needs discipline, if he is not to waste his talents. So he proposes that the three of them work out a summer school, a focused way for the boy to learn some useful things. He should not work so hard that he feels burdened, but he should do some good reading, learn more about his computer, and, this summer, begin studying music. If he can get a few other kids to join with him in these projects, so much the better. But the father will check in on him, talk over what's working and what isn't. The father is gambling that the boy would rather work, learn, feel the satisfaction of growing than lounge around bored. The father is betting on the excitement that intellectual curiosity can generate. This may make him an unusual parent, but since he is a setup for what I want to say about our instinctive searches for God, I'll assume that he could live on your street, is not a complete foreigner.

We seek God whenever we cast about, dissatisfied, for better options. The boy is burdened by his boredom, but if he learns how to overcome it, what draws him out of boredom and into intrigue, he will have gained wisdom for more than a summer. He will, in fact, have begun to take charge of his own humanity, direct his own growth. We make our selves, fashion much of our own humanity. We are different at the end of a summer where we swam an increasing number of laps than we would have been if we'd stayed on the lounger. The summer that we learned to read music still stands out. The visits to two old factories in New Hampshire, converted from textiles to book publishing, return in memory year after year, as does the dinner in the country inn, where the baby carrots were the sweetest we ever tasted.

The narrative framework, the story, that makes the forays of a summer into a search for God does not come from a boy of nine. He is simply casting about, trying to lessen his pains and increase his pleasures. The narrative comes from adults intrigued by the centrality of learning. If we human beings are the species that by nature desires to know, then knowing, learning, and expanding our world are our central plotline. How many people now accept this classical Greek view of human nature is uncertain. Our culture in the northern, developed nations does not focus on wisdom, gaining a sense of the whole of life, as rigorously as classical Greek culture did. But those among us who still examine human experience, who continue to agree that money and banking do not exhaust our human potential, remain likely to end up close to Plato and Aristotle in underscoring meaning.

The great moments in human experience are the times when our minds and hearts, our souls, take wing. We go out of ourselves in rapture at a beautiful landscape, a beguiling child. Or we solve a significant problem, taking delight as the solution becomes clear. Or we touch the soul of another person through love and feel embraced back. We need not leave the world of flesh and blood. We can be gazing across a wineglass, a spot of marinara sauce on our chin. But the significant movement, action, energy is that between two sets of eyes, two spirits on the verge of tumbling into new arroyos. The moment when we fall in love, first see our newborn child, or receive our long-sought degree can demarcate, organize, a dozen, perhaps hundreds, of other moments. What made it special, decisive, is hard to say, but almost always it was the flash of meaning.

We knew, as the experience went forward, that things would never be quite the same again. We sensed that we were involved in an exodus, if not a passage to a promised land. Old things were passing away. New possibilities, demands, realities were riding in. It was exciting, and frightening. But it was life, vitality, something more human than what had ruled previously, something worth suffering. One need not think oneself religious to have this experience, embrace the conviction that expanding one's sense of reality, meaning, is a key to the human vocation. But one cannot persevere in searching for meaning, trying to grow in mind and heart, without coming in sight of the crux of the world religions: the mysteriousness of the human vocation and condition, the plain fact that "it," the whole that seems implied, is too much for us. I think that it is legitimate, if not necessary, to call this mystery God.

RECEIVING GOD

The nine-year-old boy we have contemplated seeks "God" inasmuch as he searches for meaning, tries to consolidate who he is. Such a search, a process, moves into the question of meaning overall, the whole pattern of evolution. Does evolution have a pattern, make a whole? If so, what is it? How does it describe the beginning, where we came from? How does it describe the end? I think that these large issues lie latent in such humble matters as the boy's piano lessons. Probably most children, most adults, do not agree, do not see large issues there. If I am right in seeing them there, then most other people verify the observation of the poet T. S. Eliot: they have the experience but miss the meaning.

They may, however, feel some of the meaning — an effect, a presence of the mysterious God who makes the meaning. For example, if the boy comes to love his laps in the swimming pool, his hours at the piano, because they satisfy his body, his imagination, his mind, he will have felt the call to meaning and found it good. In his satisfaction, he will have sensed a vocation to grow, as in his dissatisfaction, his boredom and frustration, he will have sensed, felt, known viscerally the pains of stagnation, wasting time. We usually receive God, get impressions of overall meaning or telltale feelings of satisfaction, in humble ways. The boy reaches one hundred laps and loves to caress this milestone. His sister makes the honor roll and so feels that her new discipline has paid off. His father finally gets a sale at the old Yankee factory he has been visiting for two years. His mother learns from the brother of a troubled hospice patient that her patient died peacefully.

These are positive, fortunate, yet still humble experiences that justify our living with hope. The mother can go back to the hospice, volunteer again, because she has found evidence that spending time there is worth her while. The father can hitch up his pants and bang on the door of other hard sells, because the crusty Yankee manager finally smiled. The sister can turn off her TV and take up her intermediate Spanish text, because she wants her name to appear on that honor roll again. The boy can work his way through a kid's version of "The Well-Tempered Clavier" and become intrigued by harmony. The inducement in each of these experiences is to continue — volunteering, selling, studying, playing.

The wider message is that good things can happen, though nothing guarantees that they will. Eventually, it can become enough that progress, growth, and meaning are possible — that the lives we live are not determined, the future into which we go is openended.

This description may work well for positive experiences such as learning counterpoint and harmony, but what about negative experiences? Do negative experiences not cast doubts about the future, the possibility of meaning, the validity of the inference that God works in our lives, drawing us forward? At the least, do not suffering and failure say that our experience is a tradeoff, that neither meaning nor absurdity is a clear victor? In that case the agnostic would be the most rational person. The best position would be the one that says, "I don't know."

In fact, this is my position, though not the whole of it. I don't know, with any claims to empirical certainty (surety based on sense perception, experience I could handle), what God is like, how God operates, even whether God is, exists, as a person. I believe certain things about God, and I find that assuming that God exists generates a hopeful view of creation and time, but I don't know any of these things the way I know that my plane was supposed to take off at 3:00 P.M. and at 4:30 is still on the ground.

What, though, about suffering and frustration? How are they compatible with a good God, service of whom would be a holy work? Your back breaks from cancer; how can you praise God? Your child is miserable from drug addiction; what demon made this world, this corrupt society? The tribes of Africa slaughter one another; would it not have been better for them never to have been born? The Serbs of Bosnia stagger the world with their depravity; would a good God not throw them right into hell? How can "God" exist alongside AIDS?

The safest policy, when dealing with matters such as these, is to stay close to how they actually unfold. When your back breaks from cancer, the pain can be excruciating. However, radiation and drugs can alleviate such pain. Thinking about cancer, human vulnerability at large, and what the religions call "redemption," you can make the suffering less terrifying. Just as the positive experiences through which we may think that we have felt the action of God are usually ambiguous, so are the negative experiences through which we may think that we have suffered from God as though from an enemy. The child brought low by drugs can provide an occasion for our growth, by making a claim on our compassion. The tribes that attempt genocide give us all lessons in what ought not to be, what cries out for rejection, condemnation, as inhuman. So doing, they throw us back on our sense, intuitive or reasoned, that being inhuman is disgraceful, while being anything like what our species ought to be requires justice and noninjury (*ahimsa*). Some of the people in the Bosnian camps gave a strong witness, clinging to Allah throughout, as some Jews had clung to their Lord in the camps of Auschwitz and Buchenwald. Some of the people in the chemotherapy room do not fear the drip of the cytotoxins. For them "what will be will be" is no simpleminded nostrum or placebo.

The reception of God on which I have been working recently takes advantage of God's not being bound to our time. What happens to us can be God's intention from heaven, the original hour of creation. Indeed, if what happens to us through flood, fire, or sickness is part of the whole ecology of creation, it has to have existed always in the creative mind that imagines that whole and brings it into being. Each cancer cell in the broken back is mysterious for being, existing, while not explaining its existence, furnishing its own necessity. Each also has an environment, functions as part of an ecological niche. Its niche, in turn, is part of a larger web. And so it goes, spinning out to the totality, the universe. We may get tired of thinking about such a gigantic enterprise, but in itself the enterprise, creation as a whole, goes its way without strain. Individual volcanoes or hyenas may strain, explode or bite savagely, but the universe that alone finally gives any individual suffering or frustration its adequate context appears simply to be what it is, to exist as it chooses or as was chosen for it.

My sense is that merging oneself with what is overall, what happens through time, so that one has little will for anything but the reality, the actual happenings, of the world the Creator has made, is the way to peace. We receive God most significantly when we give God carte blanche, permission to deal with us as God finds best. We are most ourselves, the creatures we would be at our best, when we allow no separation between what we want and what happens. We understand "what happens" to be the "will of God," what in the realm of events actually unfolds after and as all individual actors make the contributions they find best. This leaves unanswered many questions about both human freedom and divine justice, but even alone, bare, it makes an important point. We can receive God each day by agreeing to the necessities in our lives, the things (cancers, taxes, events in Asia) that we did not manufacture. We can say yes to God, welcome God, by accepting the bodies, minds, biographies meted out to us. We can do this all the more impressively when such bodies, minds, or biographies cause us pain.

SERVING GOD

The beginning of serving God well is saying yes both to the sovereign reality of God and to what we consider God's will for us. At the head of the book of service is written that the divine mystery is the foremost wonder, reality, in any life, and that any creature, reality less than the divine mystery, finds itself best, does its best work, by trying to assist God, help move the divine plan forward, advance the divine intentions. There are two aspects of this position on serving God that I want to describe. One is how the conviction arises that God is the primary reality and treasure. The other is how we get our best impressions of what God wants, the divine will or plan.

On their way to the conviction that God is the primary reality, many saints (Augustine comes to mind) have asked questions of creation. Gathering together their confusions and frustrations, they have quizzed the natural world, trying to determine whether anything in it could still their restless hearts, give their troubled minds peace. Would contemplating the stars do the job, as the Magi thought? Was Job right in asking God to emerge from creation, defend creation against all in it that went wrong? The Buddha proposed a different interrogation. Laying it down as given, something beyond dispute, that all life, all existence that feels, is suffering, he assumed that this suffering came from karma.

Karma is the debt, the inertia, the baggage that every action done without wisdom, flowing from desire, incurs. Because of karma, most creatures go through an endless circle of rebirths and redeaths, suffering in each turn. The Buddha grabbed desire as the nettle. If we stop wanting, needing, trying to achieve, we take away

the hold that karma has on us. We duck and let karma go flying
over our shoulder. This very challenging view of spiritual combat
is like an Augustinian interrogation of creation in that it probes
ordinary experience and reports back that nothing (in the karmic
realm) brings the human being the satisfaction for which it longs.
Anything that we invest with the aura of a god or savior turns
out to be an idol, a cheat. We have to turn aside and find a different order of reality. We have to realize, take to heart, the stark
truth that old age, disease, and death infect everything that we can
handle.

The primacy of God connects with this inadequacy of creatures.
When the creatures answer Augustine, saying, "We are not he,"
they are only telling the truth. The implication, though, is that
"he" whom Augustine sought, whom the Buddha sought, whom
any of us troubled or inspired is seeking, is not a creature, limited
as we ourselves are, not something that we can handle. Either there
is a God who is uncreated, unlimited, reality in a mode utterly different from ours, or the universe, the world of space, time, and
ideas, makes no complete sense. Moreover, partial sense will not
do. It is illogical: Why should the mind stop its inquiries when it
gets to such crucial matters as the starting point of evolution and
the end? Partial sense is also impotent to heal our deepest ache
and sickness: Why are we not whole, good, happy? The intellectuals who try to make agnosticism the end of the trail, rather than
a hut along the high meadow, have miles to go before they are
done. We can do more with the mysteriousness of our situation
than reason makes possible. We can probe the affective conditions
for work and love, Freud's two components of mental health, and
come away open to faith, Bernard Lonergan's "knowledge born of
religious love."

A healthy sense of the priority of God, of the premier claims of
the divine mystery, therefore often arises in tandem with, as an effect of, an inquiry of creatures. Having found that nothing created,
obligated to outsiders as we ourselves are, can provide us the satisfactions, challenges, purifications our spirits need, we can accept
the challenge of dealing with reality of a different, uncreated order,
which reality virtually by definition is God. Even if we accept the
weight and splendor of such a preeminent divine reality, though,
how do we determine its will for us? What allows us to say, with

anything approaching confidence, that God wants us to do this such-and-such, avoid that other such-and-such? This is a pressing question inasmuch as we read newspapers telling us that so-and-so felt inspired by God to shoot abortionist X, or bomb Zionist Y, or establish in Waco a community waiting for the end of the world. It is also pressing in our own lives if we are wrestling with what to do about aged parents, or what kind of work ought to be our life's commitment, or how the stroke of our spouse ought to affect our daily routine.

At the end of the hunt, I believe that we find our hands empty. We have no certainties about who God is or how the divine mystery would have us operate. Yet we can have faith, trust, and hope that when we try to do what is rational, what detached good sense says is fitting, we are serving, obeying, the divine will for us. For example, if our spouse has suffered a stroke, we are right to assume that God wants all involved to try to rehabilitate her. We do not surrender to the will of God properly by forgoing physical therapy, appropriate drugs, any of the other helps that human ingenuity has developed for people suffering strokes. The same for neighborhoods suffering from crime and agricultural sectors suffering from bad weather or foul economic conditions.

Our first sense of the will of God ought to be that God wants us, expects us, to use our common sense, work our brains hard, strive as individuals and groups to work things out — imaginatively, reasonably, fairly. A few phenomena, patterns of suffering, stagger us by their huge proportions — AIDS, for example. Most others we could lessen greatly if we simply used our heads and cooperated generously. In two days bright people free enough to act reasonably could solve the matter of partitioning the former Yugoslavia. The relief of Rwanda could begin tomorrow if Tutsi and Hutu could be rational. It is not the obvious will of God that people slaughter one another like crazed animals. Quite the opposite. The very likely if not obvious will of God is that people treat one another justly, with ordinary fairness.

At some point, we have to accept the fact that the divine plan for creation includes awesome amounts of irrationality and evil, but this does not mean that individuals seeking God's will can locate this will properly in tribal vengeance or fundamentalist jihad. Only acts of nature impose themselves as necessities beyond the control of human beings. Most of the disorders in our personal lives, as most of the injustices among the nations, stem from human folly.

If this is so, then serving God well is often going to require putting up with human folly. We have to take to heart the patience of God, who does not blast fools away but waits, and waits some more, for them to come to themselves and stop being so stupid. God is the father in the parable of the prodigal son (Luke 15). God is the long-suffering sponsor in our own lives, writing check after check to bail us out. We do well to try to imitate God by being patient ourselves — with our children, our colleagues, even those who do us injury. Agreed, there is a fine line between patience and indulgence. Often we have to decide whether to let a bad performance go uncriticized or make it the occasion for a kick in the pants. But wise adults, it seems, overlook many foibles and follies, saving their criticisms for times when not to intervene would mean abetting significant wrong — for example, injury to others.

I remember telling a superior that a colleague was doing damage by getting drunk and exposing himself. The superior did not want to hear about it. That was irresponsibility or cowardice, not patience, because it indulged injuries to other people, hurt the common good. So there is a need to distinguish the time for patience from the time when waiting would do damage. Nonetheless, the God who made the world to run in aeons remains a model of patience, willing to wait upon the freedom of messy creatures like ourselves.

PURIFYING INTENTION

The good worker labors with a pure intention, a good conscience. This is both necessary, if one is to interact with the holy God well, and exemplary — a sign to the troubled nations, a witness to the tribes who slaughter outsiders, the developers who rape the land. The better our work for human development, the less our service of ego and hype. Human development is both physical and spiritual. People need bread, but they also need roses, poems, concertos. So apparently simple a matter as getting food to starving Somalis in 1993 shows that many peoples despise the physical needs, realities, of even their close neighbors. The warlords and thieves who took food from the mouths of starving children had the impurest of intentions. They wanted to prosper materially, and they did not care that their thefts were killing hundreds of children. What one ought to do with people so undeveloped morally, so corrupt, is hard to say. Many ancient authorities, including the Bible, allowed, even prescribed, killing rogues — bandits, criminals — because they were a menace to the common good. When people acted inhumanly, they forfeited their right to freedom if not life. If they would not abide by the mainstream mores, taken as deep values rather than superficial rules or political correctness, they ought to be forced to move on, realize they would never be welcome.

I have been pondering a case of mainstreaming that may bring this matter of purity of intention home with a bang. A grammar school in New York proposes to put a child with multiple sclerosis and an operative IQ of fifty in a regular second-grade class. The child will have her own attendant, but the attendant will not keep her from screaming for hours on end. This situation seems so bizarre, so opposed to any reasonable sense of the common good, that it reminds us how imbalanced some people can become about the rights of minorities. Out of a good instinct to help a child afflicted by nature cruelly, a school has gotten itself into a horrible bind. It has created a situation in which the good of one person outweighs the good of twenty-five others, surely an irrationality. One wonders why the parents of the child who screams are not content with schooling more suited to her special needs, but such a wonder soon comes to grief. The parents stand beyond the appeal of reason, but buttressed by some laws. It would be cruel to call them selfish, but only the truth to say that they are myopic. It is hard to imagine their intention being pure, though the New Testament reminds us that as we judge we shall be judged.

I find that ideology, political correctness, is the great impurity of our time. Though we have had gross objective lessons in such impurity from the recent Nazi and Soviet regimes, we have not taken them to heart. The reality is that any substitution of ideas for actualities, tangled life on the ground, is gnostic — a flight into fantasy. The parents of the screaming girl, and the ideologues who support them through a rigid commitment to "mainstreaming," try to blink away objective reality, the way things actually are, but of course they cannot succeed. The effects of the girl's constant screaming on the twenty-five other students are as real as the effects of sunlight on the flowers the class is growing. One cannot disregard these effects, in good conscience or pure intention. One cannot cover them over with partial truths about the benefits of mainstreaming for the healthy and normal. The tragedy in situations such as these is that most of the suffering is unnecessary. The child afflicted with the IQ of fifty deserves a special education on the academic side with social supplements. She should indeed have the chance to interact with other, normal students, but not at the price of destroying their academic environment. Only an ideologue, a rigid partisan of ideas rather than realities, would insist on creating a situation where the rights of one outweighed the rights of twenty-five. Only a town amazingly gutless or guilt-ridden would allow that situation to go unchallenged.

Under God, for God, the common good is the great goal. When we speak well of either Israel or the church as the people of God, we imply that the grace of God, the action of God for human welfare, is social. Yes, God deals with individuals in their special circumstances, but the goods of the earth exist for all the people of the earth. The resources of the church exist for all the members. Leaders of the church forget this elementary truth when they fashion their different ranks and sets of privileges. One of the craziest aspects of the "high" churches is the grossness with which clerics feather their own nests. Equally, one of the most striking irrationalities in international affairs is the diligence with which the haves keep their feet on the necks of the have-nots. If purity of intention means loving one's neighbors as oneself, keeping one's own ambitions and share of the pie modest, then purity of intention is hard to find among those who hold power.

Power does indeed tend to corrupt us, defile our intentions. That we remain affluent, or in charge of church doctrine, or the parents of a pathetic child being mainstreamed becomes imperative. We cannot let God be God and do for us what God wants through ordinary reason. We will not be detached, rational, sensitive to the freedom that our mortality offers. Because we all die soon, it ought not to matter greatly whether celibacy remains in force in the Catholic Church or the United Nations boggles at using the word "genocide" to describe the actions of the Bosnian

Serbs or the Tutsi Rwandans. It ought only to matter that many Catholic churches have no priests or that thousands of children are starving because of selfish warlords. It is tragic that countries with the power to stop such latter sufferings do not have the will, the purity of intention, to do so.

For the individual religious worker, you and me in our efforts to bring the cause of God forward, the lesson is clear. The more we can set aside self-interest and serve the common good, the likelier we are to be doing God's work. God's "cause" is not esoteric. It does not depend on special revelations, seeing the Blessed Virgin in a tortilla. It depends on common sense, basic virtue, the golden rule of loving our neighbors as ourselves. It is patient, as any understanding of evolutionary history shows God must be. It is balanced, as any tally of the destructive effects of unbridled passion demonstrates. The biblical God is "compassionate and merciful, long-suffering and abounding in steadfast love." The Buddha is compassionate, gentle, but utterly realistic. Jesus laid down his life for his friends. These are all reminders that purity of intention takes us away from the grabby selfishness of karma, the narrow narcissism of sin. Purity of intention, freedom to follow the best of our inspirations, takes us out to a large view of creation where God shares being generously and asks us to imitate her by dealing with our fellow creatures well.

EASING ANXIETY

In the course of trying to purify the intention with which we work, we are likely to encounter anxiety. Many human beings worry, act from less than a tranquil spirit. So a friend who is a lawyer takes it upon himself to rework our medical arrangements because he has been worrying that we won't get good care. Or a parent butts into his son's battles with a coach because he fears the boy won't get a fair shake. Sometimes interventions such as these are appropriate, but more often they are not. More often they say more about the person intervening, butting in, than about the objective situation.

The good religious worker, the person likely to be serving God's cause, God's intentions, collaborating well, is slow to butt in. After the disasters of colonialism, we know that the best aid is usually the quietest, the least intrusive. There is no white man's burden.

There is no cultural imperative. Indeed, there is no right to impose the gospel or the Torah or the Koran or the Buddhist Dharma. The most that pure workers, truly religious people, tend to do is make an offer. Preaching, they offer glad tidings: taste and see the goodness of the Lord. Gathering alms, they turn them over with no strings attached. Let the needy determine their own priorities. Give the aid as directly as one can, avoiding the obvious bureaucratic gougers, and then write it off. It was good to give it and no later misuse of it will take away that goodness. It was right to give it peacefully, with no anxiety about its fate.

I have been surprised at how many people seem driven to stick their noses in, seem determined to have a say. Your business is their business because . . . because of what? Usually the answer they give is, "Because I care." Sometimes that answer is both accurate and pure. Often it is not. Often it couches a need, a desire, to make a difference, throw one's weight around. I think of the retired pastor who loves to be consulted. I think of fragments of peculiar sentences dangling around the word "mentoring." In Erik Erikson's schema of the life cycle, the need to be needed dominates the middle years. There the task is generativity, producing fruits that show one's X has marked a good spot. But the need to be needed is tricky, as any honest older person knows. If this need is anxious, sweaty, panicked, it will squirt away into mischief. If the person doing the mentoring or leading the enterprise does not maintain pure hands, the appearance of freedom in the work of the apprentice, or in the supposedly independent committee, will be a fraud. Anxiety opens a straight path to manipulation. The more a person needs to feel in charge, not only consulted but heeded, indeed revered, the less helpful, healthy, that person's advice and help actually are.

Consider the case of birth control, spotlighted regularly by worldwide concern about population growth. The Roman Catholic Church, my Christian group, has become almost frantic in its efforts to muster political support for its idiosyncratic position that "artificial" birth control (for example, use of "the pill") is immoral. This position has gained few adherents outside the Vatican, so Vatican officials have concentrated on another front. Many non-Catholic groups have serious doubts about abortion, especially about the use of abortion as a contraceptive. By implying that any program of family planning will move from artificial contraception to abortion, Roman Catholic leaders have created an effective smokescreen. It is easy to make a clear distinction between contraception and abortion, but it is not in their interest to do so. Thus in my view they act with an impure intention, more concerned to wield power than serve the truth. Patronizingly, they assume they know better than the people whom programs of family planning would serve.

Indeed, if standard newspapers such as the *New York Times* are to be believed (a large if), at the UN conference on world population held in Cairo in 1994 Vatican officials did not scruple to discuss alliances with fundamentalist Muslim regimes, even those sponsoring terrorism. Some Catholic authorities are so fixated on abortion, so anxious and unfree, that they resemble Dostoyevsky's Grand Inquisitor, who thinks he knows better than Jesus. When they think they have the power, as for example in the case of the ordination of women, such authorities do not hesitate to try to stop debate. To their disgrace, many have been slow to deal with the scandals of pedophilia in the ranks of the clergy because that might diminish their moral authority in the area of sexual mores. All in all, lately I have found in the actions of too many leaders of my church a depressing likeness to the Pharisees with whom Jesus had to battle constantly.

The trouble with the Pharisees, as the New Testament presents them (perhaps unfairly), is that they have little faith, and so their motivation is impure. They are anxious to uphold the many laws that had come to direct Jewish life in the time of Jesus, but they miss the heart of the matter. They want a stolid, unthreatening status quo, in which they hold considerable power. They do not want a living God, able to raise up saints from ordinary stones. They frustrate Jesus terribly because their hearts are unclean. He pipes them a merry tune, and they will not rejoice. He gives them a dirge, and they will not mourn. He cannot please them, and soon he stops trying. They want only their own importance, like too many prominent religious and political figures of our own day. The obvious better posture before God, that of John the Baptist, seldom comes in for mention. Far from being concerned about his own status, John wanted to decrease in visibility, wanted any increase in visibility, success, influence, to accrue to Jesus. John was only the friend of the bridegroom. The popes are only the servants of the servants of God. Would that anxiety and egotism did not mock these traditional slogans so frequently. Would that more religious leaders showed holy faith like that of John.

Reason, the rights of which I have touted regularly, can show us what is sensible, the apparent common good. However, to trust that what is sensible will prevail often enough to make our common human venture good, we have to go beyond reason, to realms unseen. This is not irrational because our drives to understand and to love themselves carry us beyond reason, into the divine mystery, but it is more than rational, a choice that reason cannot guarantee. Because of the possibility that God will do good things in the future, we move ourselves forward. We trust — that what happens happens under God's control, as God chooses; that our efforts to second what happens, agree to what is, express well our creaturehood. We are not the lords or ladies of creation. We are simple peasants, ordinary proles. This is as true for popes as shopkeepers. None of us has ever seen God. But any of us can trust God, trying to write God a blank check. Though our bones break or our village fall into chaos, we can let God make the final accounting.

In this horizon, death becomes a liberation. The fact that we are mortal, sure to end in what cosmic time labels a very short while, can spring us free. If we can come to grips with our mortality, or any other profound manifestation of our createdness, we can quiet most of the anxiety that threatens to mottle our intention. We can stop trying to play God and limit the freedom of others (the sin characteristic of patrons, matrons, and patriarchs). We can finally see the arrogance in trying to ride, often roughshod, over the consciences of others. At best, we are unprofitable servants, depending on the grace of God for any success. At best, we recognize our own thorough neediness, and so we work as though everything depended on God and pray as though everything depended on ourselves.

DISCERNMENT

When we work to determine what God wants of us, how we are to play our role in the developmental plan that we associate with our Creator, we take up the task of discernment. We are trying to discern, descry, clarify the divine will. A long tradition of work on this problem has produced several notable rules. First, this tradition assumes what I have been saying about purity of intention and common sense. The less the bias of the individual worker, the greater is the chance for a pure service. The individual should want what God wants more than any personal agenda. What God wants will boil down finally to what happens. We may want a remission of cancer, but it may not happen. We may want a new job, a healthy child, the preservation of our parents' marriage, or a new government in Mexico, and none of these may happen. If our prayers that God's will be done have been sincere, we shall be able to accept this apparent frustration or rejection of our desires. We shall realize that "the will of God" is a mysterious entity, not something we shall ever comprehend. However, we need not comprehend it in order to accept it. Like Job, we can enter our protest, then surrender our will, then pick ourselves up and try again. We can give it our best political shot and then accept the results of the election.

In addition to purity of intention, wanting what God chooses to make happen, the tradition of discernment includes a note on encouragement. For people trying to do what is right, however inadequately, discouragement is a bad sign, a lure not to be taken. Whatever tells us that we can't do it, that God doesn't care, that nothing matters — that is our enemy. We need not say we can do it, or we are sure God cares, or we know how soldiering along can make a difference. We need not try to sing ragtime when our spirits wail in Sheol. But we do have to try to keep our spirits up, hold on for the day when the clouds may depart. We do have to make hope our friend, a state of soul we will defend to the end. In part this is a matter of mere honesty: no one can tell us the future, deny rightly that God is able to work good things through apparent evils. In part it should be a function of our relation with God, our history of dealing with the divine mystery.

We relate to God whenever we deal with the more, the surplus, the limitless I-know-not-what constituting our awareness. Human intelligence takes its light from the unending horizon of what is and can be. To be and to be intelligible to God coincide. Mind and existence, reality, overlap intimately. Thus if we find, as a matter of fact, that there is more to reality and possibility than what we can grasp, we have, as a matter of logic and honesty, to place brackets around any debilitating discouragement. We may have to say that the data on multiple myeloma are sobering. Only a small number of people survive four years (after diagnosis). But neither these data nor their realization in our own case (our dying within the ordinary parameters) needs be the last word. What has our dying, indeed our whole experience with multiple myeloma, taught us? Are there any ways in which we are wiser for having had to deal with this enemy in our marrow? Perhaps we can see no ways, but probably we can see some. Probably we are wiser for having suffered through a fate we would (rightly) not have chosen. Probably all the temptations to discouragement, depression, will seem at least sometimes to have been lies.

A third staple in the traditional rundown of how to discern the will of God is to think of the action of God as gentle rather than violent, encouraging rather than discouraging. This third staple therefore dovetails with what I have said about rejecting discouragement and insisting on hope. It also ties into the need for a pure intention because as long as we are trying to manipulate history, make our time serve our will rather than the will of God, we are moving against the grain, fighting the Tao that carries the ten thousand things.

Ideologues are egregious, stand-out fighters of this type. By insisting on their private, peculiar Marxist, feminist, African-American, Republican, Democratic, or other dogmas, they try to bend reality to their own wills, imaginations, agendas. It does not work. As Eric Voegelin has said, human beings will not live by depravity alone. Each generation, each person, has an inalienable orientation to reality, what is actually so. Eventually this orientation breaks through the cant of the ideologues, the tired slogans and correct political positions. Eventually ordinary members of the church say that the institutional line on birth control, race relations, the ordination of women, or liberation theology makes no sense. The day that happens is a coming of age, a confirmation with or without benefit of sacramental ritual. The person coming to grips with the nakedness of the emperor, the tubby whiteness of the official position, is now an adult. Good leaders, spiritual directors, want adults, not children. They rejoice in the maturation of conscience. Bad leaders fear mature consciences because such consciences threaten the leaders' power. The theology here is quite Johannine. The light shines in the darkness. The darkness has never comprehended (embraced, contained) it. Bad people hate the light because their deeds are evil. Good people come to the light, that their deeds may be seen in God. God is light, in whom there is no darkness at all.

The final thesis of discernment that I want to emphasize is this alignment of what is divine with what is truthful, full of light and love. If God is not light and love and life, it makes no sense to believe in God, try to serve God, try to hang on when God seems to be the enemy. Our souls have played us false. We have assumed that justice, beauty, kindness, and the like are the best things, and we have been mistaken. Fooled by our own spirits, we are bound to blush. If any of this should be so, we do well not to become criminals.

Discernment depends on a firm commitment to the goodness of God. In dark nights and clouds of unknowing, dealing with God anneals the commitment we have made. We struggle to keep our course through the storm, not to lose our way in the desert. We struggle to remember that *all* flesh is grass, not just our own. It is human to wonder, doubt, struggle. It is simple honesty to feel overwhelmed. God is always greater. We are always small. Surrendering ourselves to God means trusting that God will not crush us. The bruised reed he will not break. The smoking flax he will not quench. The theologians insist that we are never tested beyond our ability to pass the test. The saints say that abandoning ourselves to divine providence is the best course we can take. Worry does no good. We should try to let nothing disturb us. On and on the good dicta go. We need only make them our own, take them to heart, to ease debilitating anxiety and receive God's peace.

LITURGY

Our topic is working for God, but God is a strange employer, so our "work" turns out to be unusual. For example, it is hard to separate our work from our prayer. When Ignatius Loyola tells us to pray as though everything depended on ourselves, he invites us to come to God fully aware of our neediness. If we have any knowledge of what we can do, compared to what the world needs, we shall ask God with full spirits to supply for our uselessness. We cannot change people's hearts. It seldom falls within our power to convert people — from hatred to sympathy, from selfishness to altruism, from greed to spare living. Many of the world's needs, the current imperatives of history, are clear. We cannot continue to use nature as we have been using it since the Industrial Revolution. We cannot continue to pollute the skies, overfish the oceans, erode the land if we expect nature to support us in the twenty-second century. We have to curb the growth of our human population. Unless we are willing to tolerate massive starvation, epidemic, and social upheaval, we have to establish a better distribution of the goods of the earth. On and on the problems go, most of them easy to diagnose but difficult to solve. Usually the difficulty is more political than technical. Usually the problem lodges in the human heart, where selfishness taints both perception and action.

Liturgy is the public prayer to which people ought to bring problems such as these as their common cause. Liturgy affords any people the chance to remember its constitutive history, refresh the key symbols generated in its past. In liturgical prayer the past becomes present. At Passover, Jews find themselves leaving Egypt once again. Christians again find themselves beside Jesus on the cross. History can reach forward and make a new appeal. The future can become more bearable, possible, because we remember that our ancestors survived the past. Above all, theistic peoples can submit themselves again to the mystery of God, asking what overwhelms them to be their friend. Inasmuch as prayer such as this is public and communal, it rearticulates what an entire community believes. The synagogue represents the entirety of Israel, not one or two virtuosi. The *ummah* is the whole house of Islam, not a few mullahs. And the church is the full body of Christ, not just the ranks of the clerics. Whoever believes accepts this given Jewish or Muslim or Christian line of tradition and wants to contribute faithfully — that person has a place in the assembly, a seat reserved at the banquet.

The democracy of the liturgies of the world religions is striking. When it comes to the heart of the religious matter, meeting God, virtually all human distinctions fall away. The sovereignty of God swings like a scythe, cutting the proud down to size. Every believer at the liturgy is a petitioner, submitting to the imperative will

of the Creator. No worshiper with the slightest bit of understanding thinks that God is partial. Any acceptance by God is a matter
of grace. That God should care for us, take an interest, is itself
astounding. What are human beings, the Psalmist asks, that God
should care for them? How could it be that God could look on Israel as the apple of his eye? Christians inherit images telling them
that the church is the bride of Christ, his beloved. Muslims inherit
images telling them that they have succeeded Israel and the church,
receiving through Muhammad and the Koran the definitive, final
revelation. The Eastern religions run their liturgies by different stories, less connected to one another than are the stories of Jews to
Christians and Muslims. But the Eastern stories bring to mind the
Buddha or Krishna, making their wisdom or love contemporary.
The scriptures chanted at the Eastern liturgies are sources of hope,
just as the Western scriptures are.

The Greek sources of the word "liturgy" make it "the work of
the people." The implication is that the first task of any people
wanting to belong to God and serve the divine program is to pray
with good memories. Such a prayer tends to move beyond petition,
asking for what the people need, to worship proper: praise of the
objective splendor, holiness, blazing reality of God. God is the one
who is fully, unfailingly real. We are the ones who weaken, die,
slip into oblivion. Yet a part of us, the one we tend to call spirit,
hungers for God, moving out of our material finitude to play in
the vastnesses of heaven. This is the spark in our clod, the reason
our flax keeps smoking. God does not quench the smoking flax.
For the saints who persevere, God tends to transform it into living
flames of love. At the liturgy we affirm again the entirety of our
religious traditions. What we believe, why we believe it, and how
eminent predecessors have embodied it pass before our mind's eye.
We are working at praising God and renewing our own faith. Until
we experience why God is praiseworthy, our faith will tend to be
tepid. When we can speak of the beauty of God as a matter of
personal conviction, we are more than halfway home.

Liturgy is not the show of those leading it. It is not a theatrical
performance. The best liturgies are transparent for prayer, leaving
the celebrants barely noticeable. I have been surprised to find that
this message, to me obvious from the priority of God, goes down
hard in some quarters. Apparently we have numerous celebrants

who want to be performers. Apparently aesthetics bulks as large
in their psyches as unpretentious faith. This is all too human, simple immaturity. Probably it will become a smaller problem as the
people involved grow up, but it is such an elementary issue that
even to have to discuss it is disturbing. Similarly, recently I got in
an argument with a young priest who marched to the conclusion
that there is no difference between God and the church. This astounding conclusion, clearly heretical, made me wonder whether
he had ever mastered the first catechism, the one for kids seven
or eight. This priest identified his caste so closely with God that
he violated the first of the Mosaic commandments. There is only
one God. All other claimants to worship, unlimited allegiance,
are idols. This includes the church, the mosque, the synagogue,
the *sangha*. It includes all countries, ethnic groups, races, sexual affines. Nothing, absolutely nothing, can rightly substitute for
God. Nothing can mitigate the divine mystery, defend us from its
awesome exceeding of our capacity to understand. The mystery
holds all our ultimate meanings, so this excess keeps us all pe-
titioners — people who ought to show up for the liturgy feeling
needy and who ought never to confuse their group, their church,
with God.

WITNESS

Leaving their weekly liturgies or their daily prayer groups, many
people trying to work for God, make their living a service of God,
feel recharged. The precious symbols of how God has dealt with
their line in the past have sealed their conviction again. They have
confessed their sins, washed their souls, retied their wandering af-
fections. Who they are has lost its wobble from their profession
of faith, again coinciding. They are Jews, elected and covenanted.
Or they are Christians, redeemed by Jesus. Or they are Muslims,
formed by the Koran. In varying degrees, ordinary life has tended
to turn their faith dull, spread over it a patina of dust. The formal
liturgy celebrated each Saturday or Sunday or Friday has restored
the sparkle. As they leave, most of the people feel glad to be what
they are. Many also feel primed to share it.

  The religions differ in the degree to which they proselytize —
try to make converts. Christians have often been zealous. Since

the rise of Christians to greater political power, Jews have seldom
tried to make converts. Most Muslim regimes have forbidden Jews
and Christians to proselytize. Muslims themselves have increased
their ranks more by conquest than by missionary activity. They
have seldom forced peoples they conquered to become Muslims,
but the conquered peoples have found it advantageous to join up.
Muslims regard Jews and Christians as different from other peoples. As "peoples of the book," the Bible, Jews and Christians have
been cousins to Muslims and so worthy of special respect.

Witness is broader than proselytizing or missionizing. To testify to the goodness of their faith, their God, people need only live
impressive lives plainly formed by their faith. They need not utter
pious phrases. They have no obligation to bring outsiders along
to the liturgy or give them lessons in doctrine. In many cases,
a simple witness through honesty and kindness is more effective.
What we are, the character of our minds and hearts, is more important, for the long haul, than what we say, even than what we
do. Talk is easy, its grace easily cheap. Action is a better index but
still ambiguous. Only what we are, the steady, median zone of our
wisdom and goodness, suggests where our treasure lies. Though it
may take some time for us to show what we are, make an accurate impression on other people, our witness finally works most
decisively at this level.

Witness, after all, runs after God's own work. God is present
in people's hearts, has created people's circumstances, long before
we come on the scene. If people feel any attraction to holy things,
the power or beauty of the Creator, that is more God's doing than
our or their own. Our role is to give some flesh to the theses about
God that believers hold. If people can see in how we live the priority of God, the freedom from idolatry, the goodness of heart that
the Torah or the Gospels or the Koran is supposed to inculcate,
those texts, and the entire religious complex of which they are the
center, gain credibility. Conversely, the greatest hindrance to faith,
taking a religious tradition seriously, is the unattractive behavior
or being of its adherents. People ravaged by Christian crusaders
were only sensible to despise Christianity. Arabs subjugated by Israelites can be forgiven for spitting on Judaism. Muslim terrorists
give the whole of Islam a bad name.

Of course, one saintly believer can gainsay a great many bad.

Let us only meet a committed Jew or Muslim or Christian whose goodness is manifest, whose wisdom puts our own in the shade, and we have to take his or her religion seriously. As I have suggested on several occasions, possibility is the key to hope. We can hope that Islam is a straight path, a way of salvation, if we see in the lives of some Muslims the possibility or the apparent production of an admirable humanity and religiosity. The other side of this coin is that we can hope that outsiders will find our way credible, possible, if we show them an admirable humanity and religiosity. This possibility, rooted in simple logic ("From being to possibility is a valid inference"), is all that fair-minded people require. If Muslim X or Jew Y or Christian Z is an admirable human being, then Islam or Judaism or Christianity may be an admirable way of life. The fact that cynics, people who are not fair-minded, may scoff at this inference does not make it invalid. We cannot force people, observers, to be fair-minded. We have to trust that God's work in people's hearts purifies enough of them to make our efforts at witness worthwhile.

The end of witness is not the conversion of X number of previous unbelievers. The end of witness, the goal for which it heads, is the praise of God. The witness, the martyr, is saying that God is the great treasure, the pearl of great price. The witness is saying that a life dedicated to God, arranged around God, is the best of human vocations. Lost sometimes in the debates of Catholics about celibacy (the church law that priests not marry) is the value of the witness provided by the chastity, poverty, and obedience of sincere "religious" — nuns, brothers, and priests under vow. Any people who provide a public testimony to the value of living primarily for God, rather than deploying their sexuality, wealth, or will autonomously, do the world a considerable service.

The problem with celibacy is not the witness that it can muster. The problem is linking celibacy with priesthood, so that only celibate males can be candidates. In fact, historically there have been many uncouplings of this link. My point here, though, is that in itself celibacy, or chastity (pure use of sex), can be a striking witness to the primary reality of God. The pleasures of working for God, dealing with God intimately, can finally exceed those of sensual satisfaction, but we (both observers and witnesses) are such material creatures that often we do not appreciate this fact. Therefore, when we meet joyous, productive people who have handed over to God their sex or money or willfulness, we are apt to take notice. Honesty commands that we entertain their argument, their witness, that God comes before all worldly goods, is realer and more comely.

DYING

The final witness is dying with faith, handing over one's spirit to God without undue regrets. This is the summary of a good testimony, responding to the most universal need. Certainly, working for God, dealing with God, ought to enliven our humanity. The glory of God is human beings fully alive. It seems right to picture God delighting in the games, the works, the good deeds of her children. It strikes a moving chord to think that God appreciates good food, good sex, fine art. In the measure that we follow a religious pathway that stresses "the goodness and loving kindness of God our Savior" (Titus 3:4), we can believe that God wants the redemption of sinners, not their destruction, that God expects us to live as passionate human beings, not untroubled angels. A balanced, profound faith, connection to the divine mystery, is therefore "incarnational" regardless of whether it speaks in Jewish, Muslim, Hindu, Buddhist, or Christian accents. It believes that God has blessed space and time, that God, ultimate reality, wants human beings to increase, multiply, fill the earth and subdue it (though not abuse it). Healthy religion gives zest to ordinary daily life, ordinary time at work or around the family hearth. Religion that flees the world, hates the world, fears or despises human flesh is unhealthy, morbid, heretical.

This said, it remains true, a counterbalancing reality, that all human beings die, many of them painfully. From the time that we have reflective awareness, sufficient reason to make us responsible, we know that we are going to die. In the course of growing up we may learn the biological reasons for death (inasmuch as medical science itself can provide them), but these biological reasons hardly explain the Creator's decision to run evolution through death. That decision remains mysterious, indeed scandalous. The universality of death ought not to take away its affront. We have done nothing to deserve death as a punishment. We are born into what

Indian thought calls *samsara,* the karmic realm, with no under-standing of why. But there it is, plain as a pikestaff: we are sure to die. Even if the first fifty years of our life run smoothly, giving us few occasions to worry about our demise, there comes a day when we realize we have aged considerably, a day when we know we ought to begin contemplating death.

For Plato, philosophy, the love of wisdom, was the practice of dying. Admittedly, Plato floated other descriptions of philosophy, but this one is pithy enough to merit study. Plato thought that through death the immortal soul might gain a greater happiness than had been possible in earthly life, when the body weighed the soul down. For Plato contemplating the heavenly ideas through which the things of creation gained their reality was the highest pleasure conceivable. Western thought about the human compos-ite, body and spirit, has owed a great deal to Plato. The biblical doctrine of resurrection — the raising of the complete human be-ing, body and spirit, to fulfillment in the presence of God — has provided another influential set of symbols. Since the Enlighten-ment, first intellectuals and then the common people in Western cultures have grown agnostic about the fate of the human being at death. Some people still believe that the person goes before God, a few other people believe that death is the end of Susie X, of Jimmy Y, and many more people simply don't know what to believe, are waiting with more or less fear to find out.

This means that the witness of believers who accept their deaths peacefully, neither mouthing pious platitudes nor raging against the darkness, can be quite striking. I have gone through the ter-minal illness of one parent and two good friends, coming away much edified by their realism and courage. Now I am in the same boat myself, dealing with the endgame of myeloma. Probably I have further lessons to learn, but at the moment the best dispo-sition, cast of soul, that grace has given me is one that makes me indifferent to my dying, both the fact and the mode. Sometimes I don't care when or how because I am content to have what will be happen as it chooses. This "what will be" I interpret as the will of God, now apparently benign, now dark and almost savage. "Though he slay me, yet will I trust him," the familiar line from Job runs. Often I cannot reach so pure a level of faith and witness, but sometimes I can.

Dying, of course, is not completely private. Most people have
family members and friends whom their dying affects. This com-
plicates the witness of dying people, inasmuch as they may regret
leaving these other people behind or causing them grief. Indeed,
sometimes the people entering upon the last stages of life can think
that this fate would not be so bad were there only themselves to
care about. It can be liberating to feel that one's own little ego and
life never mattered a great deal, in the cosmic scheme of things,
and so that many of the burdens, the responsibilities, that one carried were somewhat false or unnecessary. But the pain of other
people is too vivid to be false. Their worry or regret is a large part
of the suffering that "untimely" death involves. Yes, most deaths
are at least somewhat untimely, though dying after age seventy-five
or so seems quite natural. But the witness that death requires of believers extends to the family and friends of the dying person. They
too have to muster the resources to deal with this sad challenge
well. As much as the dying person, they have to agree to what will
be, say that bowing to the will of God, however apparently bitter, is fitting and just, right and helpful unto salvation, as a Latin
liturgy used to say.

Karl Rahner, whose theology of death has been quite influential, speculates that death may afford us the opportunity to sum up
our lives and ourselves, so that we can say to God a definitive yes
or no. We never have the opportunity prior to death because we
can never see our motivation fully clearly or take our full selves in
hand. Freed of the opacity consequent on having a body, we might
at the passage of death finally see the proportions of our relationship with God accurately and agree to how God has played out
our life—finally see that, for all its imperfections, our life has been
good, well worth living. Rahner is too wise to enter into details
of such a speculation. Not for him any extrapolation from near-
death experiences or mystical reports, such as those in Julian of
Norwich's *Showings*. But his basic proposition is intriguing, and it
presents death as attractive, inasmuch as death may be the opportunity to quit this halfling existence we usually endure, this always
mottled way of being, for something truly whole.

Beyond such useful theological speculation, though, lie the comforts of the traditional creeds. Muslims believe in divine judgment,
to separate the just from the unjust. They believe in heaven and

hell, the Garden and the Fire. The good Muslim can hope for eternal happiness with Allah, as the good traditional Jew can hope for blessedness in the world to come. The summary of Jewish faith developed by Maimonides, the prince of medieval Jewish thinkers, includes belief in an afterlife. For Christians, the Creed is plain: "I believe in the communion of saints, the forgiveness of sins, the resurrection of the body, and the life of the world to come."

These traditional convictions, along with their correlatives in Eastern religions (*moksha,* nirvana), can be precious. The person trying to die with faith, so as to make a last, unpretentious act of witness, can draw considerable hope from them. If you have ever been anointed for death, or experienced an analogous sacramental ritual from a tradition not Christian, you know that through such a ritual history lays tender hands on your afflicted body, your frightened soul. In dying you are not going through something new, unprecedented, idiosyncratic. You are simply ending, more or less conveniently, where all those born of woman end. You have always been dust and unto dust you are returning. In its very sobriety, its absolute freedom from bullshit, this truth can cheer your soul, making you free. You just may be able to die with empty hands, no clinging, and so tell a few other people who need to hear it that freedom is our common destiny, the sweet-smelling apple pie that says we are nearly home.

Chapter Four

Loving God

OVERVIEW

In this chapter I complete my sketch of a healthy relationship with God. Freud offered the opinion that people are healthy if they can love and work. Whatever their pains or depressions, if they can summon creativity and affection, their machinery, mental and emotional, is working well. I have considered working for God, laying considerable emphasis on the purity with which the best workers offer themselves to their divine collaborator. In this chapter I deal with loving God: how the divine mystery can become the staff of a person's life.

My first consideration under this heading is the knowledge of God, the anticipation, encoded in the restlessness of our hearts. Augustine, but other saints too, including the Muslim holy people Rabi'a and Rumi, have longed to enter the divine embrace. They have felt that nothing earthly could satisfy their longing, give rest to their restless hearts. Rabi'a decided that she had to pass beyond her own satisfaction, striving to love God only for God's own sake. If her going to hell, the Fire, would praise God, to hell she wanted to go. Rumi likened himself to a reed torn from its natural site in the river bed. In the world, devout people would always feel uprooted, deracinated, cast adrift from their fundament. Rumi's poetry brims with figures of love, images of his passion for his Creator. The Sufis whom he influenced found in this poetry a strong counterbalance to the legalism that the Islamic Shariah (guidance) could develop. Much like the Hasidim counterbalancing the Jewish scholars of Halakah (the law), the Sufis stressing the love of God helped round ordinary religious practice out, make it more affective and human.

Rumi loved to contemplate the works of the Creator, the near-
ness of God in creation. My second consideration, creation, takes
up contemplation of his sort. If we look upon the natural world
sensitive to the mystery in its depths, at its core, how do we tend
to configure the apricots and German shepherds, the sand and
the surf? The epistle of James (1:17) has the figure of good gifts
coming down from a Father of Lights. The Hasidim loved to contemplate the sparks of divinity spread throughout creation. Either
way, the Creator seemed connected intimately with the things of
the natural world, the events of human history. The God who
made the world in the beginning had not cast it off, left it on
its own. Through grants of being or acts channeled by covenants,
God continued to operate in space and time. The sun and the
moon reflected the divine glory. Creatures told the alert, those sensitive religiously, much about the power of God, the beauty and
constancy. If the stars continued in their courses, year after year,
so must God, the one who put them in their courses. If the seas,
usually steady, pacific, could send wave upon wave, sometimes
swirling in storm, so could the being, the personality of God be.

Salvation, my third topic, differs from creation as repairing the
car differs from putting it together on the assembly line. God the
savior is a healer, a reknitter of broken bones. Human beings seem
unable to operate with the errorless grace of cougars and dan-
delions. We take years to get together our emotions and reason.
Eventually we have it all over the plants and animals in creativity,
inasmuch as we can build swimming pools and helicopters, but we
make many mistakes, both individual and social. The messiest blot
on our worksheet is the wars that we generate century after century. John Keegan's learned study *A History of Warfare* makes the
case that war making has become a cultural entity in its own right,
alongside art, engineering, medicine, and others. War is no mere
arm of diplomacy, not so simple as just a violent, determined way
of dealing with a recalcitrant foreign country. War seems to stem
from a deep-seated human aggression. In the awesome destructive-
ness of modern warfare we see how great is the rent, the tear, in
the human soul that the savior has to heal.

Certainly, God saves us from the wrath that many religious
thinkers have imagined human injustice and cruelty raising in the
Creator. Divine grace, forgiveness, reworks the abuse of reason

and love generated by sin. But salvation also bears on the physical
ecology (the state of the land, the waters, the air) and international
justice. It works for the poor, keeping them going. God the savior
is God the mender of broken nets, the repairer of broken fences,
the surgeon resetting bones, rechanneling veins and arteries. When
people forgive one another, make a new start, fashion zones of
peace, they show the good effects of salvation. When they find
hope and love, they should thank the divine Spirit.

My fourth topic, glorification, bears on the love that the Johannine Jesus had for his Father and also on the love that the saints
enjoy with God in heaven. If "grace" is the watchword for the
generosity of God in history, "glory" is the word for what God
does to consummate grace, how the favor of God looks when it
can flower undisturbed, unimpeded. "Glory" suggests a splendor
of light, a humanity shining. It calls to mind the angels at the tomb
of Jesus, explaining why it was empty. Jesus talking with Moses
and Elijah during the "Transfiguration" (Luke 9) is a glorious figure, in the interpretation of the evangelists for once showing his
heavenly light. The resurrected Lord featured in the first chapters
of Revelation dazzles both John of Patmos and the reader.

We human beings are bound to associate glory with God. God
is light, in whom there is no darkness at all. God is light because
God is love, the source of creativity, the fire of ardor, and the ice
of blazing intelligence. No crystal cathedral, the heaven of the Johannine Jesus takes its light from the Father and the Spirit, who
with the Word delight in one another endlessly. The glorification of
the saints, the 144,000 commissioned to sing the praises of God,
derives from this Trinitarian delight. The symbolisms of other religious traditions, such as Buddhism (for example, Hua-yen), can be
equally evocative of light, glory. The point for our forays into the
love of God is the luminosity of spirit to which lovers of God can
feel called. If often the journey seems dark and painful, now and
then the heavens open, the sun blazes through.

Fifth, lovers commune, overflowing their boundaries, washing
away many of the distinctions between mine and thine. They make
common cause, common life, common goods. The communion between religious people and their God shares many of these human
qualities. God has sworn to be faithful, as in a marital covenant,
compact. This fidelity means, for the biblical God, a presence in

history through which divinity reveals its name steadily. We can commune with the Lord of history through prayer and ministerial service. When we go to the depths of our spirits, or the farthest cast of our minds, or the need of our neighbor, we can find a holy presence to whom we can speak, to which we ought to listen.

This presence knows what we want to say before we formulate it. Usually it responds, speaks in its own fashion, by changing our spirits. If we came scattered, fragmented, often we leave put back together. If we came frightened, wanting to give up, usually we leave resigned, even courageous. The sacramental religions (Hinduism, Christianity) can focus communion such as this on icons. Their statues of Krishna or Mary can fix the desire of the believer, the need, on forms become dear through years of contemplation. Then communion is an expression of a life shared with God as a friend — the other half of one's soul.

Sixth, mysticism is the direct experience of the divine mystery. It is less something that the saints pursue than something that God grants them. Mysticism occurs in all the principal religious traditions. Some believers regard it as the peak of religious practice, but others note that the great founders (Buddha, Confucius, Jesus, Muhammad) did not require it. They were more interested in people's taking their teaching to heart and filling it with love. The mystics show us the peaks and valleys of loving God. They are more dramatic than ordinary believers, full of ecstasies and dark depressions. The love of God with whole mind, heart, soul, and strength heads for the mystery of God inevitably. Only a little fair-dealing with God shows that we are always involved with much more than we can comprehend. The mystics realize this more vividly, experientially, than the rest of us. They are the advance scouts reporting back on how the expedition goes up ahead.

Seventh, crucifixion is a symbolism prominent in Christianity but applicable to all lovers of God. Suffering for God is not inevitable, but it seems to happen more often than not. Either the lover of God becomes strange in the eyes of ordinary people and so ends up a figure of fun, or the yearning for God filling her heart makes ordinary life oppressive. Sometimes the lover breaks down, physically, and must lay this at God's door, to negotiate the justice and meaning. Other times the lover of God laments over the sins and sufferings of the world, taking what may be God's own view. The heartsickness that parents feel when the life of their child becomes a shipwreck, a shambles, may occur in God. God so loved the world he went out of his way to offer the world salvation, a pathway to new beginnings.

Those who suffer have a special claim on God, becoming like Job and Jesus. God has threatened to turn their taste for life sour and can be pressured to explain why. Usually God does explain why, though strictly speaking one who creates the things of the world from nothing has no obligation to render an account to anyone outside divinity. Usually, however, God shows the meaning that a given crucifixion may carry by making the person's life different, better in some ways, for the painful experience.

My last two considerations are resurrection and abiding. The love of God brings us into intimate contact with a God who is deathless. As communion grows, the saints seem taken up into God's life as well as God's cause. Hidden in God, their lives may begin to partake of the divine immortality. The more closely they become identified with God, the more likely this process of immortalization, divinization (*theosis*), becomes. Hard as it may be for outsiders to accredit, the death of the saints seems to postulate a resurrection. They know that their redeemer liveth, and they hope, even suspect, that soon they will be living with him.

According to the Johannine writings, we abide with God through the presence and action of the Spirit whom Jesus sends after his resurrection. His disciples find through their faith and love the Father, Son, and Spirit who constituted his own community. In other religious traditions, those who make progress along the path come to love the path, make the path the place they long to be. Thus Confucius spoke of hearing the Way in the morning and in the evening dying content. Thus millions of Buddhists have loved the Dhammapada, the little sutra (sermon) of the Buddha that makes the ethical life clear. Where we abide shows where our treasure lies, what we consider precious. For theists, nothing is as precious as divinity itself, which is glorious with goodness and light. So the Johannine advice is plain common sense: stay where life seems best to you, reality most beautiful. Stay, abide, where you find yourself to be most faithful, full of hope, empowered to love as you have been loved.

THE RESTLESS HEART

The mind tends to come upon God, discover the realities that make "God" a serious possibility, by grasping contingency. Realizing that all limited beings depend on other limited beings, the mind asks whether anything unlimited, independent, exists. Relatedly, it asks whether the ecological network of limited beings can exist, make sense, without an anchor in necessity. The heart ventures into the same area of necessity, being without dependence, but by way of affection and value. What can we love that will not fail us? Where is the goodness that corresponds to our passion to find a beauty without spot or wrinkle, a holiness that is not marred? A few people experience God directly, in moments of peak spiritual satisfaction. They are surprised by joy or feel that the mystery of the world is fully benevolent. Most people falling in love with God or living out a romance with God make do with humbler experiences — small insights into the passingness of everything human, brief times when they feel forgiven their sins and washed clean.

The love of other people (both the love that we give them and the love that they give us) is important to satisfying our restless hearts, even crucial in most people's lives, but in religious people it does not substitute for the love of God. Certainly, God can use, work through, the love of our parents, our spouse and children, our friends, but if we have tumbled to the mystery of God, we can continue to long for communion with God heart to heart, for vision face-to-face. God is not a reality, an agency, that we can replace with nature or the self or society. No effort to reduce God to something limited will succeed. The human heart awakened to its full desire finds that it is restless for the infinite, the unlimited, the purely holy. Even when it accepts and loves icons of divinity, statues and paintings that invite the senses into liturgy, the deepest passion of the soul is for a God who is power and goodness unbounded.

The unity of the two great commandments, love of God and love of neighbor, lies in the sameness of the love. When we love God, the openness of our spirits to the limitlessness of God allows us to include everything that God made and loves. When we love our neighbors as we love ourselves, fulfilling the golden rule, we find that the wonder of our neighbors is a straight path to the realization that they exist as gifts, offspring of God.

Usually love follows knowledge. We recognize that something is good, and we begin to love it, go out to it with affection. In dealings with God, love can be more directive than knowledge because our hearts can deal with God more roundly, wholly, than our minds. We can feel an urge to shut down our minds, let our hearts do the talking, more importantly the listening. We can learn why *The Cloud of Unknowing* and other classics of "negative" (apophatic) mysticism urge using a simple mantra (for example, "God") to stabilize the mind while we send darts, arrows of affection, into the divine immensity, which has settled over our minds like a cloud. Our love, the desire and admiration and obedience of our heart, is the coin we can always use with God. Regardless of how we feel or what we think, we can love God, in bad times as well as good. Bad times are not easy, and we may have to grumble before God, even accuse God of hurting us. But we need "only" make our primary want what God wants and we have the knife capable of cutting through any Gordian knot of pain or disappointment.

Our dealings with other people can profit from our considering them as analogous to our dealings with God. We can be more indifferent to the outcome of a given relationship, freer to let the other person respond as seems best, because we have given God a carte blanche. We can realize that the other person is not God and should not have to bear our need for salvation. Be the other person our spouse, lover, child, or friend, the more we can wait upon his or her self-revelation, the better our understanding and love are likely to be. The analogy with loving God even includes the precedence of love over knowledge. The knowledge that serves us best in intimate relationships is "connatural" — one gained through living with the beloved, being together in a variety of seasons. The biblical equivalent is sexual knowledge. Adam "knows" Eve sexually, and the result is children.

We can also love the poor, the sick, all the sheep without a shepherd. We have to be careful not to romanticize this love or make it a goad to ideology, but in some people it can take over the heart, leading to wonderful service. A deep spirituality such as that of Simone Weil can bring a person to identify the cause of God, the religious claim on the good heart, with helping the working poor. Ministries such as that of the Little Brothers of Charles de Foucauld begin with simply living alongside poor people, in his case Muslims. The more that missionaries of any faith can live with the people they want to serve, the more credible their witness tends to be. Sometimes it is nearly impossible for Westerners to live as poor Indians or Latin Americans do, but every effort to separate one's religious message from the cultural wrappings it has in one's own native land is worthwhile.

There should be in the United States an American Buddhism, as there should be in China a Chinese Christianity or Islam. Loving the people who have yet to hear about the good news, the Torah, or Dharma filling one's own heart requires loving their free acceptance of it, their working it out in cultural terms that make it salvific in their own neighborhoods. Just as we should believe that drawing closer to God enlarges our freedom, so should we strive to enlarge the freedom of all the fellow human beings we are moved to love.

We will not gain rest for our hearts until we come to term in God. We will, however, experience moments of respite, refreshment, significant peace, if we try to work well for God and pray regularly. Freud was shrewd in making love and work the key human needs, but by omitting prayer he showed himself to be but another intellectual embarrassed by religion. The human heart has a need to love unrestrictedly, to bow low and worship, that is at least as strong as its needs for human love and work. Nazism, totalitarian Marxism, and Maoism have shown us perversions of this need for worship, complete commitment. Fundamentalist Islam and Christianity can be all too like Nazism and Maoism, so disrespectful of reason and moderation as to be crazy. The restless heart ought not to sponsor, encourage, a demented intelligence. It ought rather to draw forth the best in us and the brightest, which it then integrates with our unrestricted love of the sole God.

CREATION

The goodness of God shines forth in all the works and attributes that religious faith associates with God. We may admire God, love the divine goodness, because we believe God to be merciful, forgiving, beautiful, holy, or any other good thing. We may also love God as the Creator, the one to whom we owe the world, including our own selves. God drew the world forth from nothingness, giving being to a divine idea. The creation of the world is an act of the divine love, God establishing shares in the full pool of reality, existence, that God alone enjoys without dependence. All of us creatures are partakers of the unlimited, divine reality — to a very small, limited degree. We are God "stopped" at a very close border, the ocean of God spilled into a tiny bay. God is the great Eurasian land mass and we are Liechtenstein or Monaco. We cannot imagine the immensity (unmeasureableness) of God. Go to the end of the universe, the farthest galaxy that the astronomers have discovered, and you are not at the beginning of God. Go to the first moment of cosmic history, perhaps fifteen billion years ago, and already God was the Ancient of Days. We do what we can, fashioning our little images and analogies, but we have to remember that we cannot even glimpse what an adequate rendering of the divine way of being would be. God is the only artist capable of painting divinity faithfully, sculpting what existing without limits is like.

That is why I have been forced to argue that we can love beyond what we can know. We can give our hearts to the unlimited divine power and goodness even when our minds have only a few clues about what unlimitedness means. The mental journey to the edge of the universe can be thrilling, leading us back to the image of God as the star-thrower. As far as the big-bang flung matter, so far has God traveled. Actually, of course, God has always been there — at any there that has ever existed. But the better picture of creation has all "theres" reposing in God. God does not fill the world so much as the world rests in God as in its matrix, its foundation and frame. History does not unfold with God as an important player so much as it occurs in God, the designer of all its twists and turns.

For people who ponder deeply the implications of creation, the existence of God is a smaller problem than avoiding pantheism — making God everything, losing the reality of creatures. Why is there something other than God? How does this something other than God manage to be? God explains himself. Divinity by definition is its own sufficient reason, its own adequate causality.

Creatures explain little about either themselves or other creatures that depend on them. We die; to the end we are ignorant; we sin; and constantly we show ourselves to be ingrates. As the heavens are above the earth, so is God different from us, other. How does the creative Other give being to creatures, our familiars? What alchemy allows creatures to participate in the sole fullness of reality? If we could answer this question, we would understand the creative action of God and so be much wiser than most of us apparently are. If we could answer this question, we would know how the divine love makes all things anew, is always creating afresh life and lesser being.

God the Creator is God working at the fine point of my soul, of the soul of my neighbor. There, where I draw being from the darkness, where some spiritual umbilicus lets me derive from the divine matrix, God is not only more intimate to me than I am to myself but more my reality, more the what and who I am, than I am. I am Peter Jennings or Connie Chung, as the world sees things. As the theistic mystics see things, I am more primarily an instance of the divine creative love, an X marking a spot where God chose to communicate the divine being. In this case, the "spot," of course, is personal, not just material. The ties between rational creatures and God seem to knot in the depths or center, where a cable of sorts brings existence into a definite space and time, a given body and soul. God may have designed most of creation systematically, for example by placing at the origins of the bloodline of Jamie Lee Z the germs of the personality traits due to surface on a big screen one hundred thousand years later. I see no reason why God cannot shape the what of all creatures from eternity through evolution in time. How God would do this we cannot understand because such a divinely directed evolution would be a function of the divine infinity. The nearer, in some ways easier, wonder is the grant of existence that God must make continually, if any creature is to stay in existence.

Secondary causes, limited creatures like ourselves, shape most of evolution, determine most of what we creatures are, our essences. Our parents take their flesh from their parents and pass it on to us. Cod beget cod in teeming millions, until stupid human beings overfish and so bring them close to extinction. Squirrels get nuts from trees that draw their sustenance from an earth watered by clouds and warmed by the sun. All this runs by secondary causality, limited agents working on material furnished them. Where does the material come from in the first place, in its primitive form? Why is there matter, this dense mode of existence, and how does it relate to thought, volition, spirit? These questions are the wonders and prods of a perennial philosophy. Generation after generation, people wanting to be wise about the most basic things, about the source and end of their world and their selves, ask them. Such people learn quickly that they cannot answer them, but that asking them, sending the human spirit traveling in their direction, is good for the soul.

It is good for our souls to ponder creation, on the way to loving the Creator behind the world, responsible for the world's design, because the world, creation, is our context, our habitat. As far as we know, the tadpole does not realize there is a world beyond the pond in which it swims. Becoming a frog, it may acquire wider instincts, but we have no evidence that they stretch to the stars. We human beings are the species that knows about a universe, from Alpha Centaurus to CD 34, the genetic spot that may prove decisive for curing multiple myeloma. We are the beings who can reason about God, can love God even though reason fails to account fully for the divine limitlessness, even though God seems to be the author of a story often cruel, full of suffering. We can surrender our hearts to the splendor of the universe, its sweep and power. We can gape at the possibility that the one who flings the stars could speak to Elijah softly, give such light to the mind of Gautama that most of Asia has seen its glow. God gives all things that are possible their possibility. God is the ground of possibility, the determiner of what might be.

Again and again we have to remember that there are no limits in God — no space, no time, no matter, no finitude, no sin. God exists in another order from what we know. God is the Creator who is not created, is not made by design. God is God's own maker, sustainer, designer, as God is the solely adequate exegete of God's meaning, any communication meriting the name "revelation." For these and a dozen other good reasons, our hearts can take fire when contemplating creation. God made all this reality, all this beauty, all this swarm of pleasure and pain, wonder and burden. We know nothing about ourselves and our world un-

til we have settled with God about creation, made our peace and
accepted our tiny place.

SALVATION

Creation tends to be the love, the intrigue, of philosophers. Salvation is the bonny child of theologians, thinkers trying to understand the implications of their religious faith. Salvation connotes
healing, repair, rescue from dead ends, dangerous paths. Inasmuch
as he saw the whole samsaric world as burning, a conflagration of
desire, the Buddha was a savior, teaching a way to escape from
the flames. Inasmuch as the revelation of Allah given through
the prophet Muhammad was a straight path leading people away
from dire judgment, onto the high way to the Garden, that revelation was salvific. Salvation is help from God for our brokenness,
forgiveness of our sins. Salvation is God in a tender mode, concerned more that the wastrel, the roustabout, the whore repent and
flourish than that harsh justice prevail.

The instinct at work in this view of salvation is that sin hurts
the sinner far more than God. When we act irrationally, cruelly,
selfishly, we go counter to our own best interests. Our best interests condense into drawing close to God. The closer we get to
God, the more fully we can be ourselves. God is the source of our
freedom, not the enemy. God is the one who lets us be — more
creative, more joyous, wiser. For sinful creatures, afraid of God,
this is counterintuitive. Adam and Eve trying to hide their nakedness is more representative. We know that much is wrong with
our world and our private lives. At the least, we know that we
have not appreciated God, seen the sweep of reality as God's ma-
jestic doing, as we ought to have done. We have been blinkered,
self-absorbed, petty. The grand spectacle of creation, the constant
parade of the animals, has passed us by. We have followed our
myopia and our self-interest into cul-de-sacs where we could not
hear the cries of the poor, where high fences kept us from seeing
the disparities in the nations' standards of living. So we flee from
God, allow distraction to be a buffer. If we came to God humbly,
like the tax-collector whom Jesus contrasts with the Pharisee, we
might pray better. God might forgive us our sins and restore our
sense of acceptance.

The traditional Chinese view of the life cycle has three vices predominating. The vice characteristic of youth is lust. The vice characteristic of middle age is strife. The vice characteristic of old age is greed. I have thought about this typology often. At each stage, the dysfunctional, sinful effort is to prescind from God, live as though God did not provide the orientation we need to develop capacious spirits, in wisdom and peace. Lust is the derangement of physical love, good eros. Strife is the derangement of justice, striving for what is right, confronting and battling what is wrong. Greed betrays an anxiety about the morrow, a failure to consider the lilies of the field, how they grow. As I have moved along the life cycle toward the end of middle age, the beginning of old age, I have collected more sympathy for lustful youth, less sympathy for greedy old age.

Nowadays young people have done well if their first thirty years have made them rational — able to choose, pursue, what reason, not emotion, says they ought. Many of the young academics I see are very bright, quite well trained, but surprisingly immature. At thirty they are far from having gotten their lives together, their personalities in order. Their educations have neglected maturation of character, so they do not know themselves well. Though they have little wisdom, they are often supercilious and proud. A teenage novice who had spent a year with a desert father or a demanding rebbe or a Zen master would be much wiser than they. Lacking such a formation, they, as most other young people, do not know how to direct their great yearning, the desire that the Buddha considered the root of all suffering.

God the savior can cool the fever of youthful passion, calm the strife of irritable middle age. The glory of God seen in human beings' full vitality is lusty in the sense of full-bodied, not ashamed of the earth, but it does not snigger, is not prurient. The right order of the mature human personality includes a hatred of injustice and evil, a willingness to fight hard against them, but it also sponsors a sense of perspective that keeps people from constant raging. By middle age we should realize that many things go wrong regularly. The most irritating of these things come from the slovenliness or stupidity of other people. As my friend the harried oncologist said once, "You can tell them what to do, but you can't give them a brain." I am preaching to myself here. After fifty-five years, I still have considerable work to do on patience, forbearance, realizing that stupidity and laziness are afflictions hurting the stupid and lazy more than their customers.

I see greed working perniciously ever time I page through *Modern Maturity*, the magazine of the American Association of Retired People. I also see folly because the horizon of most of the pieces is pathetically secular. People within sight of death are treated as though retirement to a life of golf and travel were the acme of human fulfillment. Sticky-fingered grandchildren (in small doses) appear more than good books or prayer. Where is the wisdom that old age has provided in the great cultures of the past? Where is the guidance that comes from seeing human affairs under the aspect of eternity? Of more interest to AARP is making sure that no one cuts Social Security, Medicare, or double-dipping retirement arrangements. I find *Modern Maturity* a pathetic, embarrassing depiction of what too many people my age and older think that a life's worth of experience should have made precious. All in all, it strikes me as a prospectus for mediocrity.

God the savior deals with all the lesions that lust, strife, greed, and the other vices can inflict, as well as with the truly profound human problems: mortality and sin. God the savior is God the holy, the mighty, the immortal having mercy on us sinful, weak, death-bound human beings. United to God, we may hope to be freed of our mortality, welcomed into the undying divine light. United to God, we may hope that the huge incapacity of our species to sustain development, because of systemic sin (wrong-headedness, selfishness), can cede to a divine grace worked almost despite our torpor, by an unobtrusive Spirit praying effectively with sighs too deep for words. God can do what we cannot do. God can save us despite ourselves. We have to want such salvation, at least sometimes, to some extent, but God can widen our want and by answering it bring us to admiration, even worship. Any of this is the doing of the God who saves us from ourselves — turns us around, reorients our souls. All of this is remarkable, wonderful, a new creation.

GLORIFICATION

Grace suggests how God works to heal human existence, bringing us from the alienations and dysfunctions of sin into the gentility of a healthy humanity, one dominated by what Confucius and Mencius called "fellow-feeling" (*jen*). "Glory" suggests the term of this process, the full transformation of the human being that union with God might effect. In Christian terms, glory becomes stable only in heaven, where the just behold the face of God constantly. Heaven is an elevation of human potential so that it achieves what is by nature beyond it: partaking in God's own life. Such an elevation occurs through the free goodness of God, who chooses to love us so intimately that we enter the divine family, enjoy appropriate measures of the light, life, and love that make God God. This intimate love is not the suppression of us creatures but our unexpected fulfillment. In what traditional Jews call "the world to come," Muslims call "the Garden," and Buddhists call "nirvana," everything good for which human beings long comes into their possession.

Nonetheless, the core of such fulfillment remains beyond human comprehension because the core is being with divinity immediately, without concepts or images or icons having to mediate our appreciation and love. In heaven God will still be a mystery because God will be God (unlimited, endless, the Creator) and we will remain limited, creatures. But this mystery could draw us into itself endlessly, providing wonder upon wonder. People who worry that heaven will be boring have not reckoned with the infinity, the limitlessness, of God. They have not entertained, given good brandy to, the proposition that God plus the universe makes no more existence, being, reality than God alone.

There is a fullness in God, a plenitude, that is like an ocean without shores, a landmass without borders. If we become citizens of God's land, sailors on God's ocean, we can go on and on. There is no limitation from time in the glorified existence of God. There is no limitation from space. The religious traditions that speak of resurrection of the body make heaven, the state of our fulfillment, material, but this is a matter freed of sickness and many other limitations — a "glorified body." The light and fire of God at the root of the figure of the divine "glory" extend themselves to the earthly partakers of divine life. Whatever is necessary for the full activation of human potential occurs in heaven, through the proximity of the creature to its Creator. Eye has not seen nor ear heard what such a fulfillment might be. The great divide of death keeps it at too great a distance for us to visit and inspect.

This means that any discussion of "heaven" is speculative, even that which occurs in the Bible or the Koran. No one has been there and brought back a map. No one can show us pictures of the yogurt the heaveners like to eat, the yurts in which they live. The best that theologians can do is try to discern the specific needs of human nature, as their religious tradition presents it, and then reason to the characteristics of the state that would meet those needs, provide complete fulfillment. For example, assuming that the Koranic figure of the Garden hints at the complete fulfillment of men and women, Muslim theologians interested in life in the Garden, life fully pleasing to Allah, have imagined flowing streams, luscious fruit trees, full-throated praise of God. Christians have reasoned that the being of God, the divine intelligence and love, is the gist of heavenly fulfillment, what the saints enjoy most, adding the specifically Christian conviction that such fulfillment flows through the sacramentality of Jesus, the Word of God become flesh. Buddhists have depicted nirvana as the freedom, the unconditionedness, that comes when the flame of desire has blown out. All the lets and hindrances introduced by samsara, the karmic cycle of death and rebirth, would fall away. The natural Buddha-nature of all beings, their intrinsic light, would shine fully.

These speculations are precious, but we err if we take any of them literally. The book of Revelation, for example, is a treasure trove of hints about human fulfillment with the Christian God, but to take the symbolism of Revelation literally is to make what philosophers call "a category mistake." Religiously, it is a species of idolatry. We are not willing to let God be God, mysterious even in heaven. We insist that God limit divinity to a line of images or practices that we can comprehend, perhaps think that we can control. No, the glory of God is human beings fully alive, enjoying heaven with zest, and so moving deeper and deeper into the infinite goodness of God, the light that has no end. The goal of human existence, as the wisest of religious teachers describe it, is the praise of the divine glory. If we ever saw, understood, loved purely even a fraction of what divinity is in itself, our minds and hearts would blaze more than the sun. God is the sole being responding to the hole at our center, the great yearning. Being with God definitively, by God's gift enjoying God's own estate, is how we were made to end.

By the same token, any valid understanding of "hell," definitive human failure, has to be the reverse of "heaven," the opposite. Hell therefore is less a matter of fire and physical punishment than a matter of losing God, not accepting God's invitation to journey through the divine limitlessness and sing God's praises constantly. We ought to be as chaste, as restrained, in our depictions of hell as we are in our depictions of heaven. We ought to apply as stern a demythologizing. The same with the matter of divine judgment. If God has a tribunal before which the dead come to be sorted into those bound for heaven and those bound for hell, we have to believe that all the works of such a tribunal square with the dignity of God, the divine justice, and the divine mercy.

God the infinite is not hurt or diminished by human sin. Any injury that God suffers is injury to which God has made himself, herself, liable. We do not know whether God's caring for creatures entails disappointment when creatures sin, exultation when creatures do well. We cannot say what God can or cannot do, be, feel. We can only cling to our conviction that God is good, providing for our welfare far better than we can ourselves. We can only keep vibrant our belief that God deserves a blank check, the totality of our trust. Living and dying with such a trust, we can hope to enter upon the glory of our Father who is in heaven and hallow his name without end.

This hope should be enough for us. We should not need to sniff after visions and miracles. There is nothing wrong with miracles and visions, and it is not our business to say whether God ought or ought not to bring them about. But they should never become more important than the plain, simple creed of our long-standing religious tradition. The Christian Creed, for example, speaks of more wonders than any alert reciter can fathom in a lifetime. The simple Buddhist ethical code known as *sila* encloses a program for great moral achievement: not to kill, not to steal, not to lie, not to be unchaste, not to take intoxicants. This is "mere" Buddhism, as the Creed is "mere" Christianity. It has no lust for signs and

wonders, no itch to be exceptional. The glory it seeks is a share
in God's own glory, given when and as God deems best. God is
its great preoccupation, not itself. God is not the thirteenth step in
its twelve-step program. God is beholden to, like to, nothing other
than God. God is first, and we come far later, far after. God is also
last and foundational. The glory of God is the lamp of which the
Koran speaks, lighting the heavens and the earth. The glorification
of creatures is their establishment, enthronement by God, to share
the divine glory.

COMMUNION

The general topic of this book is how best to deal with God,
the mystery in which we live, move, and have our being. In this
chapter I deal with loving God, under the conviction that people
who can work for God effectively and love God passionately are
healthy religiously. In taking up "communion," I turn attention to
the bond arising from our love for God and God's love for us. I
deal with the union, the joining of minds and hearts, the common
cause, that religious (unrestricted) love creates.

As we become familiar with God, friends, and lovers, our lives,
existences, overlap with God's increasingly. We become more interested in the causes of God, for which God invites us to work.
We also become more aware of God's interest in our causes — the
persnickety stomach that disturbs our sleep, the child who won't
grow up. If our communion grows, deepens, we can come to feel
easy with God, relaxed. This will not make us disrespectful. We
are not likely to forget who is the Creator and who the creature.
But it will make us joyous, carried by a sense that we are not alone.
We have a friend in the highest of places. The best of arms extend,
open to embrace us.

Communion is a simple activity, a reality with few parts. It
proceeds mind to mind, yes, and heart to heart, but the fullest
communion is being to being. All that we are flows out to God. As
much of God as God finds good, as we can receive, flows into us.
The classical figure of "participation" captures much of this communion. We take part in the life, the being, of God. God takes part
in our life, our being. Certainly, God has always been in us, and we
have always had our being in God. But that natural relationship

fades. To the fore come the freer, more personal overtures proper to people in love. Much of what traditional Christian theologians have tried to understand through a distinction between the natural and the supernatural becomes clear when we study communion with God.

Theoretically, God can create us, give us being, without opening the divine heart, inviting us into the recesses of the divine knowing and loving. (Whether God actually does this — create without personal disclosures, personal stakes — is debatable.) The revelation that the prophets have considered a great favor, the drawing aside of what veils divinity, has been personal in this way. The Lord instructing Moses on Sinai, like Allah teaching Muhammad in the desert night, put divinity at risk. Despite the daunting sovereignty that God has shown, he had to know that his message could be, eventually would be, rejected — ignored, cut down to manageable size by clerks and dullards.

Where does human ignorance of God, sinful neglect of the one thing necessary, leave God? How must it feel to be a Creator whose creatures show little gratitude, a savior whose beneficiaries keep falling back into sin? If the saints, the human beings who try hardest to measure up to the goodness of God, God's love, are pitifully few, must God not wonder, in God's own way, whether the whole arduous, painful process of creation is worth it? The Bible shows God regretting that he made a species that could degenerate to the level of Sodom and Gomorrah. The flood that only Noah escapes is punishment for human depravity. These are anthropomorphisms, of course, as are my musings about the feelings of God, but communion with God seems to sanction them — to make God more like us, more vulnerable.

Communion with God does most of its good works by making our love of God more intimate. It is easier for us to imagine this intimacy as God taking our interests to heart than as our taking God's interests to heart, but perhaps the traffic travels both ways. Perhaps when we pray simply, personally, being to being, God feels freed of some burdens. Yes, God is perfect and suffers no burdens. But by choosing to make history, drama in both cosmic and human time, God has taken on works fraught with burdens, frustrations. Whether what frustrates us also frustrates God is hard to say. On the one hand, we want "God" to be free of frustrations, so that there will be one place in reality (in fact, the source of all the rest) that is independent and unmarred. On the other hand, communion with God shows us a divinity that puts off its privileges, rolls up its sleeves, comes down in a housecoat. God has a homey side, something companionable, a willingness to linger over a second cup of coffee.

Moses, the friend of God, got special treatment because of the intimacy that he developed with his Lord. God arranged for Moses to see all of divinity that a human being could without perishing, being blasted away by the divine holiness. Abraham nagged at God, became a nudge, for the sake of the few just people in Sodom. Job kept badgering God for justice. In all these cases, God seems to have endured human lobbying good-naturedly, almost with pleasure. True, this depiction of God says as much about the writers of the Bible as its says about God. Nonetheless, the peoples of the book have found it a winning portrait as, generation after generation, their communing with God has brought them close to the divine heart.

The New Testament has similar images, similar invitations to trust God naively, as a child trusts a good parent. If we ask God for bread, we will not receive a stone. If we, evil as we are, know how to give our children good things, how much more God? God is like the father of the prodigal son, like the woman sweeping her house to find a single coin. God rejoices more over the return of one child lost to sin than over ninety-nine dutiful others. The remarkable intimacy with God that Jesus shows in the New Testament, epitomized in his use of "Abba" to address God, holds out a model for our own communion. We may vary the usage of Jesus, choosing, for example, to address God as "Imma," Mother, but we should make our own the cast of mind that Jesus exhibits, both audacious and trusting. God must become our God, a frequent visitor, a beloved friend. It is not enough for God to be the generic Creator or savior. We have to feel that God made us uniquely and that God wants our healing because we are the apple of God's eye, the darling daughter or son. All of this intimacy comes into play through our communing with God. Less and less is there mine and thine. More and more we let God love us, stop squirming away.

I remember hours spent in dark chapels, where the smells of candle wax and incense set a mood conducive to prayer. Indeed, the flickering lights of votive candles made the darkness quick, mysterious. The call, the possibility, concerned communion. We could share our days, God and I. I would smile at the conceit more than worry it. For if it was a perfection, a good quality, for a human relationship to sponsor easy sharing, why not prayer? If I could go across the street to end the day laughing with a few good guys, why not good feeling in the chapel? As my life unfolded I did not develop these warm intimations as generously, as wisely, as I should have, but they have never left me. Whenever I behold the Johannine Jesus communing with his Father, many such intimations return, rekindling a small fire.

MYSTICISM

Mysticism is the direct experience of divinity. God, the ultimate reality, makes divinity present, known, as a force transforming the mystic's being. Mysticism proper, in contrast to the many accommodated uses of the term, is more passive than active. The mystic undergoes the action of God, the divine operation. What reason may have said about the full priority of the Creator in the creature-Creator relationship becomes experiential. God lets the mystic know something staggering about this priority, calling forth awe. The mystic cannot say all that the experience contained — words fail to render it. But the mystic can say that it was unmistakable, indubitable. With or without graphic images, impressions on the senses, God has let the mystic know more of what divinity is like in its own right than reason alone ever could. Blaise Pascal feeling God as a fire in his breast is a good example. Though he was a scientific genius, perhaps also a philosophical genius, a few moments experiencing God directly changed his life. What neither science nor philosophy could deliver came gratuitously through prayer. He learned that his God lived, was not the inert, distant, cold God of the *philosophes*. He learned that his religious kin were Abraham, Isaac, and Jacob — the patriarchs of the people God had chosen to deal with personally.

Mysticism is germane to my topic of loving God because it brings a consummation of sorts to both prayer and work. Inasmuch as our work is a service of God and our prayer is a pursuit of intimacy with God, we can experience mystical moments as

times when our efforts bring excellent results. The irony or paradox is that our efforts themselves create nothing in the mystical
moment. At best they prepare us to receive God, if God should
choose to visit dramatically. The communion that can develop
steadily through faithful contemplative prayer may flower in mystical, experiential awareness of God, but that is for God to say.
For us to say is that we really are trying to use our time and material resources well, for the works of God, and that we do actually
show up at our prayer station on schedule, to share all that we are
with God.

Intellectuals can make this twofold statement, apply this twofold assessment to their lives, and so can simple religious people.
Mysticism is no respecter of social class, age, sex, race, or even
religion. God raises up children of Abraham, believers, when and
as God chooses. The prophet Jeremiah received his vocation with
dread. It was not at all what he wanted. The same with the prophet
Jonah, sent by God to preach repentance to hated Nineveh. Jesus
would have passed the cup of crucifixion by, and Muhammad
wondered at first whether the revelations that created the Koran
were not signs of his going crazy.

Mysticism therefore is nothing sugary or titillating. It is the effect of God's unmuffled voice, God's fighting for our hearts with
the gloves off. The wonder is that all mystics don't faint away,
and the fact seems to be that often the mystic does. The body
cannot bear the intensity of the encounter, so the mystic swoons.
With further experience the body toughens, but feeling God directly is always dangerous. God is demanding that the mystic
leave ordinary human ways of perceiving, thinking, willing, which
are piecemeal. Proper dealing with God is simple, whole, as is
divinity itself. That is why love, communion from the heart or
core of one's being, is the best preparation for mysticism. That is
why working for God doggedly, without questioning constantly
the worth of one's work, takes believers in a mystical direction.
Mysticism involves what we have called connatural knowledge:
awareness gained from living with another person. Still, love and
faith are more to the fore. If the mystical relationship is to mature, the mystic has to let God be God. This can entail a loss of
ordinary supports, normal bearings, that is almost horrible in its
despoliation.

In language developed by John of the Cross, but applicable to many other mystics, the dark night of the senses is the despoliation of our feelings, so that we can deal well, faithfully, with a God we cannot see or touch. Consolation and desolation continue to visit us, like tutors with useful lessons, but the Spirit of God is our primary teacher. The Spirit leads us out of the fleshpots of Egypt into the desert where there are few sensible shows to distract us. Part of this journey is simply ordinary human maturation. We leave the land of children, human beings who cannot do what they ought because it is unpleasant physically or emotionally. We enter the land of adults, human beings for whom reason weighs more heavily than emotion, the common good takes precedence over our personal pleasure or pain. Unfortunately, by these criteria a large fraction of the population adult chronologically is not adult psychologically or religiously. Therefore, weaning people away from sensate living is often countercultural. It is also a significant blessing.

Beyond the night of the senses, however, lies the night of the soul. Here the darkness is deeper, more demanding and frightening. We realize, through the action of God in our depths, that everything about us is impure. Without denying the crucial biblical proposition that God looked on creation and called it good, we begin to see that our own sinfulness runs deep, like a dangerous fault line. We forget the preeminent reality of God and the blessings God has lavished upon us. We grow weary of trudging along, enduring considerable pain, and so we consider throwing the whole venture of religion in the dumpster. God lets us know that we are always going to be ignorant, left in the dark, and at first this knowledge depresses us. Later we can find such ignorance consoling, in part because it implies that no one else knows what God is either. No atheistic hotshot or dogmatic pope has been mailed the divine dossier. In the beginning of the dark night, though, we probably will experience our ignorance as another humbling facet of our finitude and sinfulness. The sin now in question is less given acts that went awry or stemmed from impure motives than a general waywardness, torpor about the things of God. The sense is not so much that we did bad things as that we are bad — twisted to the roots of our being.

The dark nights make it clear that God is hard for us human

beings, a more than adequate challenge. Yes, I have said that time in the chapel can be enjoyable. Yes, sometimes we can leave the dark night of the soul by contemplating the prodigal father lavishing acceptance on the wastrel son. Nonetheless, many holy people report slugging along for years with little sense that their fidelity, which they would never call exceptional, pleases God. Most days God seems indifferent, if indeed it remains credible that there is a God. The lesson seems to be that God is too real, too omnipresent, to be extraordinary. God is the suchness that Buddhists praise, the being at which philosophers wonder. The Christian God is as ordinary as human beings suffering, as regular as visits to the cancer ward or the mental hospital.

God wants us to see what is there, right before our eyes. God wants us not to harden our hearts when she speaks. Everything is grace. Nothing is ordinary. The voice of God whispers that our sin does not repulse God, drive God away. God is compassionate and merciful, as testify the turn of the leaves in the fall, the quiet after the storm, the goodness of sleep at the end of a trying day. However, God will not be satisfied with a little corner of our lives, a Sunday or Sabbath fraction. The "jealousy" of God, as the Bible calls it, is the requirement of a realistic lover that we see things, live with things, as they actually are. As they actually are, God is the puppeteer and we are the puppets. God moves all the strings entailed in creation, somehow without destroying our freedom, and we dance our wonky routines. God is always greater than what we imagine, what we trust. Mysticism is our direct experience of this divine majority, priority, "excess."

CRUCIFIXION

Crucifixion is a good symbol for the sufferings in creation with which we must come to terms if we are to deal honestly with either God or serious other people. Biological evolution is not a pretty picture, a good bedtime story. The species have evolved through trial and error, feast and famine, the law of the jungle. Human beings have been brutes longer than they have been civilized, and the history of human beings shows nearly incessant warfare. The vast majority of human beings have died young by today's standards (before fifty), and most have lived hard lives focused on bare survival. We moderns are the anomaly in human history. For all that purists sing the praises of the vegetarian diet of some prehistoric peoples, we live decades longer than they and with many more amenities.

Indeed, we have a population problem, globally, because of our success at curbing infant mortality. For the first time in history, human beings can expect that a newborn will survive. True, whole continents have yet to share in these advances fully, and disproportionate numbers of women and children linger on the economic margins, where comforts are relatively few. Nonetheless, the affluent northern nations have been able to shift many of their sufferings from the basic level of material survival to the more rarefied realm of the psyche. Our prosperity has allowed us to become narcissistic, self-concerned, babyfied as few of our ancestors could be.

Recently my wife and I stopped at a vegetable stand and dealt with a tiny, wrinkled Japanese woman and her quick, Americanized granddaughter. The corn, beans, onions, and garlic that we bought were exquisite. The woman reminded me of gardeners we had watched at one of the Shinto shrines in Kyoto. I suspected that farming had been the work of her family for generations. She was cheerful and properly proud of her produce. In her wrinkles I could count both the blessings and the curses of a stratified society, a nearly karmic determination that baby X would be a gardener, a farmer, or a shopkeeper, as members of her family, her *jati* (Indian caste), had been for centuries. Such a system places a high value on stability, continuity. Only when all members are in their proper social places do the custodians of the system feel good. But the price of such a system can be high: for the majority, hard toil, generation after generation. On the other hand, the rewards can be rich: satisfaction from good work, peace from living with limited expectations.

The Eastern cultures influenced by the notion of karma counsel acceptance, dispassion. If we give up wanting, we can avoid disappointment. The cultures that shaped Western civilization placed the wellsprings of suffering in sin or fate — notions as mysterious as karma. Karma is a postulate, an assumption. One cannot prove it empirically, and it leaves several crucial questions unanswered. Where did this moral law come from? Why do we have desire,

ambition, if it is bound to bring us suffering? Sin is also a postulate. Where do we get the norms that tell us that murder and theft
are wrong, inhuman, irrational? How are we able to choose and
act irrationally, from selfishness rather than objective response to
the common good? If we choose fate as our explanation for suffering, we make no great progress. Who or what writes the script for
fate? What sense does it make to call randomness, chance, Lord of
the evolutionary universe?

The sufferings that come from earthquake, fire, flood, and tor-
nado are bad enough to make us question the wisdom of the
Creator. The sufferings that come from human malice, from the
hatred of the priests and Pharisees, can be harder to handle. According to the New Testament (a source with an axe to grind), bad
people like the Pharisees who resented Jesus hate the light because
their deeds are evil. The light, the good conscience generated by
living honestly before God, requires that they change their shame-
ful ways. We all tend to flee from the light, avoid the truth of God,
when we feel that our lives, our selves, cannot bear close scrutiny.
With time, this dishonesty gives us consciences, moral selves, that
are callous, insensitive.

Thus Pontius Pilate went along with the murderous intent of
the enemies of Jesus because the death of a Jewish peasant meant
nothing to him. He served a brutal empire, intent principally on
preserving its own power, so he knew brutal means intimately.
The wonder for Christians is that God could let this happen. How
could the Father of Jesus give him a stone when he asked for
bread? The answer lies in the Father's resurrecting Jesus, but before we get to this answer we ought to pass through the dark night
of the crucifixion of Jesus. Roman soldiers nailed the hands and
feet of Jesus to two crossed pieces of wood. They drove metal
spikes through his flesh (sinews, blood, bones), causing him un-
speakable pain. He died as a criminal, despised and derided. His
life was an utter failure, as Pilate (the representative of the obtuse world) saw things. As the New Testament sees things, the
priests and Pharisees thought it expedient that one person die to
keep Rome from repressing the entire Jewish people for political
agitation or sedition.

As the religious person sees things, God was wrong not to save
Jesus from the cruelty and pain of the crucifixion. Equally, God

was wrong to let the Meccans run Muhammad out of Mecca, to let the Israelites drive Moses to distraction in the desert, to ask Abraham to sacrifice Isaac. These are things that we would castigate in human beings. Why should we not castigate them even more in God? Elie Wiesel has pushed this point in several of his writings. The rabbis in his Nazi camps put God on trial and find him guilty. But then the rabbis move on to pray. They have passed judgment, according to their human standards. Now they must submit their judgments, their human standards, to the divine mystery.

I think that this double movement is precisely what honesty requires of us when we encounter suffering reminiscent of the crucifixion of Christ. We have to condemn the evil that we see, laying it at the door of the human beings who perpetrate it. We also have to give voice to the doubts that evil raises in us, our wonder about the justice and wisdom of a God who allows crucifixions, Nazi camps, the mutilation of little children. But then, in a second movement, we have to acknowledge that we do not have the understanding or the goodness to pass judgment on God. Following Job, we have to confess that we are but dust and ashes. We ought not to excuse God facilely, especially if we are not suffering physical pains ourselves. But we should remember that "God" oversees, is the architect or owner of, an infinity of beings and a vast multitude of cosmic events, some of them destructive. Thus Jesus himself chooses to follow the apparent will of God that he suffer crucifixion, and Muhammad turns his exodus from Mecca into the beginning of a new, Muslim era centered in Medina. Wiesel extends his concern from the Holocaust to the phenomenon of hatred worldwide, as a generation earlier Martin Luther King Jr. extended his concern from racial justice to the immorality of the war in Vietnam.

The names of suffering are legion. Each name calls into question the goodness of God. When natural or human evils tear us apart, we are right to ask God for an explanation. Where we go wrong often is in not listening for the explanation God offers. We assume that there is no explanation, no defense that God can muster. Or we assume that God doesn't care about the likes of us, even when we writhe and weep. My experience is that this assumption is premature. If we can endure the silence of God and not keep tearing at our sore hearts, we may feel a balm, an unknotting, a massage, that brings us relief. What remains unexplained intellectually — the physical and moral defects of creation — may become bearable emotionally. In asking us to trust him, God raises the stakes of the game considerably. Do we believe that the maker of heaven and earth moves by love, benevolence — believe it sufficiently to hand our little creaturehood over into his keeping? Do we believe that God seeks the flourishing of the creature, even the sinful creature, not its punishment or demise?

These are easy notions but difficult realities. The person facing a five-year sentence in prison meets them in different garb than the physician in the third pew. But the fact remains: many lives fall apart, crack up, assume the shape of a crucifixion. Does this mean that they lose all sense, should be cast aside as bad trips? Or does it mean that God is deeper, darker, than what glitters in crystal cathedrals, what appears effortlessly in advice columns? God is not our teddy or our manservant. God is not a nanny for little princesses or a maid. God lives all alone in the divine splendor, answerable to the likes of us not at all. God can do with us whatever God chooses because without God we are nothing. Thus John Donne asked God to batter his heart, make him pay attention — a prayer incautious but fitting.

RESURRECTION

Resurrection is a response to the question boiling in crucifixion. If God raises human beings from death and takes them into the divine light, death is not the end. The final say about human existence, history, is positive. What had been a tragedy becomes a comedy, the triumph of grace. The stories in the Gospels about the resurrection of Jesus imply that it inaugurated a new creation. The messianic age, the kingdom about which Jesus preached, had begun dramatically. The intent of the Father to offer divine life, vitality stronger than death, had taken hold of time, human flesh, and set it on a new track. Henceforth, human beings could hope to pass through death into an intimacy with God, a sitting at God's right hand, like that of Jesus.

Resurrection of the body was not a new notion. The Jewish culture that Jesus imbibed used it to picture the future. But res-

urrection did not determine the structure of Jewish faith as it came
to determine the structure of Christian faith. The New Testament
offered good news based on the resurrection of Jesus. For the authors, the Spirit of Jesus was alive in the midst of the church. The
sayings of Jesus gained their full resonance only against the back-
ground of his resurrection. The miracles attributed to Jesus became
signs of the divinity he had possessed from the beginning. What
emerged clearly in the resurrection had been present all along, explaining why no one had ever spoken as he had, why he alone
had the words of eternal life. He was Lord of the Sabbath because
the Sabbath was his own law, now seen to be less significant than
the welfare of human beings. Before Abraham came to be he was,
outside of all time and turmoil. Thus the "I am" marking God
in the book of Exodus became the characteristic expression, the
signature, of the Johannine Jesus.

All this high Christology, interpretation of Jesus as divine,
occurs to the writers of the New Testament, becomes not just legitimate but ordinary, because of the resurrection. The "I am"
sayings are laughable, even demented, unless the Father displays
Jesus as his equal. The miracles bring thoughts of magic. Grant-
ing that the Father has raised Jesus, however, the confidence of
the writers of the New Testament makes sense. Within the lifetime
of people they themselves have known, God had broken history
apart. Now only the hopelessly cynical, the Pharisees of succeeding
generations, could allow no such interventions by God.

Christianity is singular in laying so much stress on the resurrection of Jesus. Eastern religions do not have the concept of
resurrection of the body, though they do speak of complete fulfillment coming from a radical break with desire. Judaism and Islam
have the concept, but it is not central, not the keystone, as it is
in Christianity. Beneath the obvious symbolism in the New Testament accounts, and the problem of verifying through ordinary
historical means an event that breaks ordinary natural laws, the
Christian community has discerned something objective, factual,
and decisive. For this reason, the Creed speaks of the resurrection
of the body and the life of the world to come, making them articles
of faith incumbent on all wanting to be orthodox (right believing) followers of Jesus. If there is no resurrection, Christians are
pitiable, as the apostle Paul discerned. They are taking comfort in

a myth, a pious tale, not something objective, solid enough to lay the weight of a life upon.

If you take up present-day scriptural studies, you will find that few scholars will commit themselves to any simplicity about the composition of the canonical writings. Most see layer upon layer of human collection, editing, and rearrangement. What if anything comes directly from Jesus himself is minimal, indeed tends to get smaller every decade. What to say about the resurrection of Jesus is a dilemma, if not an embarrassment. The accounts in the Gospels are statements of faith, certainly, but what credibility they have apart from an antecedent commitment to Christianity is hard to determine.

I respect the labors of New Testament scholars, and I like the sobriety, the restraint, that I associate with the best of them. On the other hand, there is a further cut to their argument that the scriptures are documents of faith — testimonies written by believers for believers. This further cut is the offer, the possibility, that the entire biblical way of life, depiction of God and Jesus, is uniquely nourishing, singularly responsive to human need, and a dozen other good things. In other words, it is possible that the "great cloud of witnesses" from the biblical generations and later has not been wrong in judging Jesus' way of love to be the consummate human wisdom. The Creed that includes the resurrection of the body as an article of faith has fed hundreds of saints, as well as hundreds of zealots, crazy people. The Creed does not remove the need for faith, struggling with the divine mystery, but it does help to specify the personal grounds for faith.

We ought not to take articles of faith as logical propositions that reason can test and submit to its judgment. Rather, we ought to locate given articles in their historical context and probe the symbolic power they have carried, both originally and later. The Jewish notion of the resurrection of the body owes much to the vision of the prophet Ezekiel in which the people of Israel emerge from slavery in Babylon like a skeleton, a collection of dry bones, reassuming flesh. The details of the New Testament accounts are touching, especially the way that Jesus deals with Mary Magdalene and Peter. Admitting, with many New Testament scholars, that these details may serve literary, theological, even polemical agendas of the authors and editors, we still can, perhaps have to, ask ourselves how the portrait of God, the delineation of reality, that they bear forth strikes us. More specifically, we can, perhaps have to, take up a task that most New Testament scholars avoid: comparing this candidate for our existential commitment, our choice of a master-story by which to interpret our lives, with the others pounding on our door.

I have never found a story more compelling, challenging, consoling than that of the New Testament. Through upbringing, with the conditioning and prejudices it produces, I have looked to the New Testament for a unique wisdom, and often I have found it. Through doctoral-level analysis, I have probed what human ingenuity can make of this body of scriptural writing, as of any other (Torah, Koran, Dharma). This probing has made it plain that there are no guarantees to be found in human reasoning about any scriptures. Only something more than human can validate our taking a master-story rooted in a scripture as our main guidance for life. Only God can make faith in God, confessional acceptance of the resurrection of the body, reasonable. Healthy faith does not violate reason, but it does go beyond it. Healthy faith reposes more in the personality of God, the character of Jesus, than in empirical data or logical argument. So, at the end of the day, the final hour of the deathwatch, healthy faith is not a gift of measured scholars so much as an offspring of our love of God, our wonder that we should ever have been invited to take part in the game of history, salvation, death, and resurrection.

ABIDING

As we wait in joyful hope for the end of our adventure in loving God, its consummation, we do well to contemplate the Johannine invitation to abide in the love of Jesus. I take "abide" to mean rest in, wiggle down into, make one's retreat, inner cabin, treasure. The love of God, which for Christians is, characteristically, the love of Jesus, is the source of our being, our reason-to-be. Without the love of God, we have no adequate explanation. To postulate that evolution simply began, and then blundered forward to the production of human beings, is to write a fairy tale much more naive than Genesis. No, it makes more sense by far to postulate or infer a God truly transcendent of the world, fully mysterious, who for inscrutable reasons decided to share divine being through an evolutionary process. This second, theistic postulate preserves the rights of the mind to keep asking for explanations. Where the first postulate, of an inexplicable big bang, hangs in thin air, the second moves off from the character of creatures. At its strongest, the view that God is the maker of heaven and earth derives from (*a*) the fact that things actually exist, combined with (*b*) the analysis that these things do not explain themselves (that no chain of limited beings gives creation its reason-to-be, its anchor in necessity).

The love of God makes all this dependence on a necessary being personal. The reason we exist is a benevolence, a good will, of a being powerful enough to say "Let there be." The power of God may be warm and hopeful. In creating, bringing forth new being, God may be like a mother pushing her child forth from her womb. In her joy that a new life has entered the world, she may forget her pains. Indeed, if she is a wise woman, she may store up this moment against the future trials the child is likely to bring. Perhaps God creates in this way, with a rush of excitement at the wonder of new being, with a searing hope that so fragile a little bawler will make it through the storms and parching heat to come. This is the love, the good pleasure, in which we can abide. At the center of ourselves we can find a license to be, letting us go forward, that is like a liturgical blessing: Go forth, have courage, hold on to what is good. The limits of our picturing the love of God are the limits of our theological imagination. God may be like a top-quality futon, inviting us to lie down and rest. God may be like a lover, taking us to herself in the dead of night, wrapping us around with smooth arms. The parent sending the child swinging into the sky, chortling with delight, may tell us volumes about God. The friend or lover keeping watch through the vigil of AIDS may tell us volumes more. We can see, sense, the abiding love of God in a thousand different places, if we have the desire and bestir ourselves. We can watch the drama of life in a shelter for battered women, a negotiation for the reduction of arms, a consultation about a new chemotherapy, as though God were a partner, claimed a stake, laid out good money for shares. There is no sensing the action of God, the omnipresent energy of the divine love, without faith. There is no transmuting the often horrible, crucifying fate of God's people (any people) into a work of love without a theology of suffering — one as deep as the experience of Jesus on Calvary.

All of us, believers and unbelievers, Christians and adherents of other traditions, abide in something. All of us have treasures, *margaritas,* on which our hearts are set. As the existential philosophers influential during the 1950s and 1960s chanted, "Even not to choose is to choose." If you say there is nothing in which to abide, no ultimate treasure or divine love, you make nothingness your prime explanation of reality. You may do this with considerable sophistication, as a Buddhist or Christian exercise in negative theology (nirvana is ineffable; no language can render God adequately). Or you may do this retractively, drawing in your horns, reeling in your hopes. Still, something (the state of the candle when the flame has blown out, the freedom from illusion that giving up hope can bring) will lodge at your center, be your gyroscope in the night.

Those who make the love of God their center and source of orientation are subject to both illusion and disillusion. They can think they have solved the problem of how to set a life securely on the path that is straight and so be reluctant to learn the further lessons that the mysterious God requires of them. They can realize that the love of God is not a rose garden, a candy factory, a clean-scented candle never flickering. The love of God can seem cruel, careless, even punishing. The move from hurt and astonishment to "so be it" can stretch like a marathon. Yet what other religious choice do we have? If we vote for a limited God unable to help us, as the best-selling rabbi advises, we have violated the first commandment, committing idolatry, adultery of the religious heart. No, far better to say that God is unlimited, other, truly divine but inscrutable, hard on her prophets and saints, than to whittle God down to our proportions. No truly religious person wants a God we can understand, carry around in our back pocket. The God we long to worship is both infinite and good, both free of any need for us and nearer than the pulse at our throats.

I do not understand the psychologizing of God, the lowering of Christology, that prevails in the religious best-sellers nowadays. It strikes me as the rawest ignorance of what the religions have said in their best moments — what Isaiah and Aquinas and al-Ghazali have known. There is no low Christology limiting Jesus to a rich humanity, defaulting on the faith of Nicaea and Chalcedon, in the theology of Karl Rahner and Karl Barth. The giants continue to know better. But the pygmies win the applause of fellow pygmies for denaturing traditional faith, diddling round the campfire or witchy circle, and they are too impure not to feel confirmed in their deviance by such kudos.

Oi vey. I sound like an old pope with a sore hip. The love of God in which I should abide is less troubled, more laughing. Ever ancient yet ever new, it takes no special umbrage at current follies. From the time of Adam and Eve human beings have been block-heads, slow to learn the abiding things for their peace. Why should things be different nowadays?

Conclusion

Why Bother with God?

❧

I have friends who have little use for religion, say they are indifferent to God. How can that be, if God is the overwhelming reality, the blazing primacy, that I have been describing? Two explanations come to mind. The first is that such people are missing the obvious, blundering badly. The second is that such people are actually dealing with God every day, though unawares.

We do meet people whose lives seem to lack depth, not be serious. They run and run but have no impressive goals. In the United States often they appear swamped by trivia. Whether or not they sigh to us about their busyness, their burdens, we find them overloaded, strung out. They are so involved in things, mired in stuff, that their spirits are cramped. No truly liberating education has given them a horizon broader than the newspaper. No contemplative prayer has plunged them into the mysteries of being, the costs of salvation. They work and they love, but not impressively. They are T. S. Eliot's hollow people, living and partly living.

Other unreligious people may outshine churchgoers in humanity. Their work may be more creative, their love more playful, their generosity to the unfortunate more impressive. In their lives, their selves, we can see both depth and beauty. They come before our mental gaze when we think of models to place before our children, goads to our own better living.

For the theologian, these people of admirable humanity are dealing with God, willy-nilly. They are saying yes to the invitations from reality to work on, fudging none of the data, to keep loving their children, no matter how ungainly. They could not tell you why they feel obliged to contribute to the building fund for the new shelter, but obliged they do feel. It is the right thing to do, and

they can spare the money. They have been fortunate, smiled upon
by fate, and this makes them inclined to help the unfortunate.
In each of these acts, feelings, of responsibility or generosity, the
people in question have flown by faith. No lawyer has persuaded
them that fidelity to the canons of science is the lawful, right way
to behave in their laboratory. No child psychologist has argued
that parents ought to love their children in good times and bad, regardless of the affection or disaffection they feel. The wretchedness
of the street person huddled against the cold has been argument
enough for contributing to the shelter. The simple doing of a few
good deeds like this without any sermons from clergy has made
the case that formal religion is not necessary.

The good secular person accomplishes most of what a reasonable religious tradition desires. People who love their neighbors
as themselves, who keep the precepts of *sila,* are doing the will
of the God in high heaven. What they lose by not thinking about
life in theological terms and not worshiping God formally is significant, but they can place this loss alongside their avoiding the
cant of much institutional religion and judge that they still come
out ahead of the game. In fact, often their problem is less with the
teachings of the church, synagogue, mosque, or *sangha* than with
the style, the way of being in the world, that it projects. For example, a clerical style, where those running the religious body think
themselves all-important, puts many good people off. A luxurious
style, where places of worship and education become sinkholes for
endless amounts of money, gives the lie to professions of simplicity,
living close to the poor.

What good people lose by not exposing themselves to a theological analysis of their lives boils down to mystagogy. Mystagogy
is the exercise, the putting in play, of the mystery of God, the
wonder-full character of creation. Mystery and wonder are not
words, concepts, prominent in serious discussion nowadays. One
can find them in reviews of theatrical productions such as *Cats*
or analyses of creative programs for children, but there they do
not carry the full weight that theology wants them to carry. This
full weight is the load that the best literature delivers, the thought-
fulness and pondering of an author such as E. Annie Proulx. The
characters in her recent novels *Postcards* and *The Shipping News*
grow on the reader, until the uniqueness of each life, and its de-

termination by a series of apparently random happenings, emerges for full appreciation. Good literature provokes contemplation: sustained, appreciative study. It holds before us characters and stories in which we may find our own condition, the simply human condition of being mortal and messed up. Good theology does much the same, though it focuses more explicitly on God. In the mysteriousness, the wonder, of the human condition good theology finds the finger of God, the patient love of the Creator.

Secular people are the poorer for not exposing themselves to good theology. They have to make do with theodicies, explanations of suffering, cobbled together from common sense. The peaks and valleys tend to escape them. They have no tools for calibrating the best moments of work or love, when the wonder of the world, of one's own life, is palpable. They have no ancient symbols to comfort them in the night, the cold, when the furies howl. Certainly, theological views can become harmful props, barricades to growing up. Any good thing can be abused, and religion is frequently. But the examined life, the truly human life that comes only by probing our foundations, origins, and likely ends, requires our sailing into religious waters. Ultimacy is the middle name of the religions. Religious rituals and myths exist because generations of people have sought to connect themselves with the universe, live in peace with the way things are. Not to seek to connect oneself with the universe, not to recognize that peace with the way things are is not inevitable, is to proclaim oneself unreflective, to characterize one's life as unexamined.

So we bother with God, slog through the muck of religion, because we want our lives to gain depth, our spirits to come in sight of wisdom. We want our souls to have their shot at holiness, reality shining without flaw or lesion. We have learned that love is the best and most trying of human experiences, and learning this has reminded us of the saying, "God is love." Religion can take us beyond such extensions of our human searching, forcing us to let go of reason. Prayer can drop mystery over our minds like a cloud. Religion can also complicate our dealings with sickness, evil, suffering, and death, even as it can smooth such dealings with solid consolations. Either way, we are better, wiser, and more tested for having entered the lists to grapple with religion. In the past, some of the most gifted people of the day gave their lives to religious practice and reflection. We do ourselves a service when we listen to what scripture, Augustine, Luther, the Talmud, and the Sufis have to say. The successors to such luminaries in our time are harder to nominate. Rabbi Heschel stands out, Thomas Merton. Those who seek usually find the solid fare they need. In my view such seeking leads to the divine mystery, leads us to love God's being more than we can imagine.

HOW TO KEEP GOING

A few people seem to live in perpetual sunshine, smiling always. Most of us have good days and bad days, times when it is easy to bless God and times when it is hard. How can we keep going through this up-and-down, now-and-then existence? How ought we to think about dealing with a variable God, a variable self, variable circumstances both religious and secular?

The best way that I have found is by not making distinctions. This is not an easy way, and often I do not follow it well, but it pleases the most faithful parts of my mind. Suppose that there is no simple sunshine and rain in God, no unqualified good days and bad. Was the Friday on which Jesus died the worst of days or have Christians been wise to call it good? Was Israel's wandering in the desert the best of times or the worst? People who tumble into serious illness, as though falling into an elevator shaft, can emerge the better for their pains. Under the aspect of eternity, whatever makes God increase and makes ourselves decrease is good for our salvation.

The point is that everything connected with God is mysterious, richer than what we can locate by our graph paper. Salvation, creation, sanctification, glorification — all take us beyond our depth; any can push us into a shaft. If we give up our attempts to control our lives, to pass judgment on how we are doing, what happens does not matter. What matters is our appropriating what happens, our sifting out the lessons God may be offering us. Naturally this is not easy. We want our trip to go well, and so we groan when we hear a tire go flap-flap or the yahoo in the pickup clips our fender. We think that something bad, annoying, has happened to us, fulfilling Murphy's law. None of this instinctive evaluation is wrong, but all of it is partial. Back at the motel or in the peace of our own home, things may settle into less troubling perspective. At the least, we have received another painful reminder that we have here no lasting city. The peace and rightness for which we long exist only with God. Until we find God definitively, we are pilgrims, trying to trudge our twenty miles each day with grace. We live by faith more than knowledge, by hope more than attainment.

In the measure that we have established a regular communion with God, the distinction between good times and bad lessens. Good times are those when our communion is most intense, deepest. Bad times are those when our sinful dullness has made God seem far away, unattractive. Once again, this deep level of communion with God or alienation from God does not obliterate the need for judgments, both analytical and practical, on other levels. The decision about the new chemotherapy remains as much a crapshoot today as it was yesterday. The wrongness of cancer or AIDS or alcoholism does not diminish. But no longer are these judgments ultimate. Only our sharing our time, our fate, with God is ultimate. Everything else is penultimate, secondary.

Down the line, where the railroad tracks leave our sight, we can intuit a convergence. If we hand over to God our caring overmuch what happens to us, most of our days can unfold carelessly. If we make the will of God, the cause of God, our great love, we can think that any outcome is providential. This includes such horrors as the wars in the former Yugoslavia and Rwanda. If they are not subject to God's providence, history is a chaos, the idiot's tale that took Shakespeare's breath away. If they are subject to God's providence, they do not become good, but they do become penultimate. God is responsible for them, inasmuch as God has chosen the order of the world, the blueprint of creation, within which they occur. Thus we can believe that God's being responsible for them means God's doing something about them — God's keeping in mind, providing for, what might redeem them.

Inasmuch as I am discussing human phenomena such as war and genocide, I should note that God has a special problem. Having made human beings free, able to say yes or no to what they ought to do, God has to respect their, our, right to do evil. In complementary fashion, we have to believe that God is wise enough to outwit human evildoers and make their sins serve divinity's own purposes. Further, we have to believe, often against our own deep pain and hurt, that God stands alongside us in our sufferings and continues to number all the hairs of our heads. We cannot see how what is happening to us — the illness or rape or financial ruin — could ever be good, but we do not have to see this. We have only to keep open the *possibility* that God is using our sufferings for purposes beyond our ken. We do not have to affirm that God is doing this, let alone say what such purposes are. Sufficient for any evil day is retaining our basic sanity, a large part of which comes down to confessing that we are not God. Because of its eloquent version of such a confession, the book of Job is considered a major work of wisdom literature. Because Ibn Abbad of Ronda (fourteenth century) had a profound sense of the divine will, his letters read well today.

The simple, deep, practical way to keep going, through good times and bad, is to make all times moments, stages on life's way, that we share with God. In the measure that we consider God to be numbering our days, meting out a providence tailored to our unique needs, we can find this way attractive. We don't have to achieve great things, as the world judges such matters. We have only to work as best we can and let the chips fall where they may. We don't have to keep our weight at 125; we have only to eat sensibly and exercise moderately. We are not the masters of our fate. In our bones, our genes, we have come from the sole Creator, to whom alone we belong fully, owe an allegiance in no way hedged.

Activists may worry that reflections such as these encourage people to devalue history and human efforts to make the world more just. The worry has good grounds, but if it is simply true that we do not run the world, have not made either the world or ourselves, the worry has to cede to a bigger reality. In fact, neither Moses nor Jesus nor Muhammad (nor the Buddha nor Confucius) became a recluse or a quietist, defaulting on public life. The social aspects of human existence are as inalienable as the natural and the personal. But all aspects of human existence shift, enter new constellations, when we try to coordinate them with a real, living God. All lose their imperative, bullying character and gain a new, pacific character because we start to see them as servants of God rather than independent agents. If creation is the free and rational work of God alone, as the biblical religions have portrayed it, there are no independent agents. Every wind and rock serves God's purposes. Every dying is the work of our sister Death.

THE GOOD LIFE

The good life is not one replete with money or possessions. It does not center in a good reputation. Even healthy children and significant accomplishments through hard work do not capture the good life, cannot guarantee it. The longevity that traditional Chinese culture has sought, and the enjoyment of creation so winning in Judaism, fall short of what religious wisdom intuits complete fulfillment to be. Only communion with God, abiding gracefully now and entering upon a glorious consummation after death, matches the span of the human heart, the reach of healthy human desire.

If so, our living with God well becomes simple. We have only to commune with God, pray to God, and work for God each day in order to move along the blessed Way, the path that is straight, the Tao directing the ten thousand things. What all the major religions have suspected — that the guidance offered by the divine mystery is like a path through the wilderness — emerges in this common symbolism. The Torah, the Gospels, and the Koran all point to a way of life. Indeed, all express what a heart ordered rightly and feet moving forward rightly look like and in practice work out to be. The Indian path of the Dharma is like the Confucian and Taoist Way in being both the wisdom handed down by the ancient masters and the road that nature itself travels. The Dharma guides people into "suchness," thinking realistically, moving with the grain of things. Similarly, if we hear the Confucian Tao in the morning, in the evening we can die content. If we apprentice ourselves to the Way of Master Kung, by the time we are seventy it can happen that there is no difference between the Way and our own will. We can want only what the Way commands or offers. We can have no self that rebels, is untoward or unruly.

The good life is that of the person whose self is integral, in no serious way untoward or ungracious. Gratitude marks such a self through and through, as ingratitude marks the self that is immature, still thrashing about pitiably. The immature, sinful self wants and wants — possessions, attainments, applause. It fears it will not exist, its little light will go out, if it is not always out selling, making its pitch. Though it is tiresome to people who know better, it may draw a wan smile from a parental God. Like the teenage daughter playing the princess or the teenage son in the sloughs of grunt-and-scratch, the self on the sell is more to be pitied than blamed. It cannot see most of the wonders of creation because its own needs hog the window. It barely suspects that the good life is selfless — carried out of the prisons of narcissism by love of a dazzling Other. Human love and creative work can prepare people for this outgoing, this ecstasis from self into a reality more objective, beautiful, and compelling. In the process, they can heal the panicky self of many of the wounds that keep it on stage dancing. But the definitive liberation is religious: taking to heart the freedom of worshiping only the sole God.

In properly religious terms, the good life follows the dictum of John the Baptist. It makes our self-concern decrease, our love of God increase. The saints move beyond any conceit that they can pass judgment on God. For them dwelling in the house of the Lord, singing the psalms of the Lord, is already beatitude, a biblical nirvana. Communion with God seems too good to be true. The obscurity of God seems only proper: How great would God be if we could understand her? This giving God the benefit of the doubt in all circumstances cashes out the blank check mentioned earlier. It has to occur honestly, from a state of soul where no grievance against God roils the waters, but when it does occur, it removes a dozen obstacles to peace.

The joy that we see in the lives of many saints flows from their contentment. They are in love with God and so feel prosperous beyond all their deserts. Certainly their ill health or the conflicted state of the world continues to bother them, but these are penultimate matters, as we have said. Much more is involved in the good or bad running of our bodies, the healthy or sick interactions of the nations, than what human beings can grasp or control. So, having done what we can, worked hard and purely, we are wise to let go. What will be will be. What God has ordained will happen. Any other clinging, interjecting of our will, or fussing to tip the scales will put us at odds with divine providence. As God respects the freedom of human agents, even when this respect leads to evil results, we ought to respect the freedom of human agents, even when they mess up their own lives. We have more right to intervene, more obligation to oppose them, when they do injury to innocent bystanders, but even there our responsibility is limited.

The best opposition to abortion, for instance, avoids trampling on the civil rights of people who believe that abortion is a valid moral option. By extension, the argument that antiabortionists have the right to kill abortionists, because the latter are killing innocent human beings, is irreligious as well as looney. In the psyches of those proposing this argument abortion has swollen so that it represents all evils, epitomizes evil pure and simple. How do we resist evil, lessen the epidemic of abortions, and point out their sickness without becoming fanatics, people trying to set their impatience in place of the divine long-suffering? How do we hate what destroys human life or blasphemes against God without losing our sense of proportion, our sense of humor, our awareness that we too have sinned and fallen short of the glory of God?

One way is by contemplating those who have lost their balance. Beware the humorless soldier, the militant ideologue. Beware the absolutist, the person limited to black and white. God does not paint in only those colors. God does not sponsor any particular political correctness. There are pro-choice people of good heart and delightful wit, as there are pro-life people. There are blacks and gays and Muslims who carry no chip on their shoulder, as there are counterparts who do. Life comes to us empirically, in individuals. Abstractions walk no side streets, pay no rents. We do not meet African Americanism or homosexuality or Islam at the market, in line at the ATM. Ideologues miss the richness of actual life, the diversity, the broad palette. The good life presents this diversity as a feast, a cornucopia, a challenge to keep broadening our horizons. If we have pried our fingers off the controls, agreed in our heart of hearts that God alone is running the universe, we will suffer fewer temptations to ideology, fewer upsets at what actually occurs empirically. Certainly, we will continue to find that some of our assumptions are outmoded, no longer match the local suchness, what seems to be so right here. But even that will not matter a great deal, for we will not be carrying the burden of omniscience, omnicompetence. We will be living as free spirits, passing through time lightly, having few positions, investments, hard to give up. There will be less winning and losing, less gamesmanship overall. What matters is not our batting average but our communion with

God. We can commune with God through both losses and times when we win. We can call either time good, if communion with God occurs.

The Christian liturgy for the Easter vigil speaks of the sin of Adam and Eve as a happy fault (*felix culpa*) — a tantalizing paradox. As noted, there is a Christian tradition of calling the Friday on which Jesus died "good" — another paradox. What seems bad, or good, from the perspective of worldlings can seem just the opposite from the perspective of the saints. Worldings are interested in avoiding pain and increasing pleasure. Saints are interested in communing with God, pleasing their Creator and beloved. Perhaps there are saints who are dour, more depressive than manic. Who am I to dictate the modes in which God can nourish holiness? I suspect, though, that the signs of the Spirit underscored by holy people prevail in most saintly personalities. These signs are peace and joy. They are deep spiritual dispositions, not just passing moods induced by good eating or exercise. They are harder to summon or find when the holy person is in pain, physical or spiritual, but they can coexist with considerable discomfort. Holy people know better than to become complacent or presumptuous. Peace and joy are gifts of God, effects of God's free benefaction, not their own doing. On the other hand, God is not stingy, a miser with his hands closed. God is generous, wanting the life of the sinner, happiest when able to slaughter the fatted calf and bid the musicians strike up. Communion with God is often a party, a messianic banquet. The body of God that we embrace is good bread, thick and savory. The blood of God, the care poured out, is good wine, dark and dry. We do not lose by handing ourselves over to God. With the saints, we can count most of our adventure gain.

WISDOM

Wisdom obviously connects itself to the good life. Wise people are those who are realistic about human existence and so have set their hearts on proper treasures. Religious wisdom makes God or ultimate reality the most proper treasure. For the religions people who are wise place God first, set their hearts on a beauty, a goodness, that is unearthly. They want a relationship that no moth or worm can destroy. They want a love that carries them on and on, infinitely. "God" is the only reality corresponding to this want. Wisdom is concentrating on God without becoming deranged, forgetting one's debts to the body, one's conditioning by space and time, one's immersion in nature and society.

Religious wisdom has its seasons, which vary as it ripens. In the early years, gurus may find it useful to impose critical controls, get quite clear what "God" can and cannot mean. In the later years it may seem better to let all such critical-mindedness move to the margins, so that love can dominate uncontested. The early years can draw on the same energy as strife to work apologetically — defend the faith, show the reasonableness of opting for God. The later years can use the approach of death to boost the primacy of God: the grass withers, the flowers fade. The wonder is not that God exists but that we do, that there is a world. The puzzle is not that some people do not trust God completely but that we don't, keep holding back. Granted a good God, all logic says that we should live carelessly, with great trust. We may grant a good God because we have known mystical moments when God took over our hearts indubitably. Or we may reach God by a generalized argument from fittingness: construing the world as the work of a divine Creator is more elegant, pleasing, explanatory than construing the world godlessly. Either way, once we have come to a good God and made divinity the primary reality in our mental life, our view of the world, we ought in all logic to make God the primary reality in our emotional life, what we long after and pursue as our delight.

Wise theists simply try to be what they profess. They profess to be the creations of an unlimited Creator. Do their lives, their daily dramas, reflect the imagination, holiness, and freedom that such a lineage implies? Creatures are improbable happenings, rational creatures most of all. The "Gaia Hypothesis" gathers together various aspects of this improbability, arguing that the uniqueness of life in the measures that we find it on earth makes the earth an evolutionary freak. What apparently happened here has no counterpart in what astronomers have yet discovered in the rest of the universe. That may change in the next millennium, but for the moment the odds favor the earth's evolution having been providential — guided with special care by the forces that ruled from the big bang to the development of *Homo sapiens*.

Religious faith does not depend on any particular astronomical or evolutionary hypothesis. While today the "Gaia Hypothesis" may seem to favor the existence of a divine providence, tomorrow new data may throw that hypothesis in the shade. Far better for religious analysts are the constant factors that shape human existence, such as our mortality and our ignorance. We all die, and none of us knows with empirical precision where we came from at birth or where we go at death. Wisdom requires us to take full account of basic verities such as these — orientations, determinants of our human situation. No president, ballplayer, bishop, or supermodel is going to escape death. None of them is going to gain God in such a way as to put God on display, let them charge five dollars and feel good for giving one to charity. The biblical walk-through that Oral Roberts has constructed in Tulsa is more humorous than supportive of faith. When the mechanical snake slides down the apple tree in Eden, one feels a surge of pity. The story of the fall in Genesis is a wonderful patch of ancient wisdom. The dioramas in Tulsa tilt faith in a literal direction that evacuates that wisdom. If Adam and Eve are not everyman, everywoman, as the etymology of their names suggests, they are stooges on the order of Fred Flintstone, cartoon characters that only amuse.

The drama in the Genesis story reposes in the human tendency to resist God, disobey God, think that we know better than God. Instead of trusting God we trust ourselves, a substitution absurd to enlightened reason. Of course, Genesis assumes that God makes the divine will known so clearly that what we are to do, what fruit from what tree we are to avoid, is never obscure. Few of us experience the moral life, the life of choices about good and evil, to be so straightforward. Yes, many church leaders would like to make the moral life so simple for us. In the best of worlds, as they see it, they would speak and we would obey without question, ideally without thought. Even when their will is good, their mentality is primitive. They confuse God, whose clear will any wise religious person would hasten to obey, with themselves, puny representatives of God, Pharisees made of the same dust and ashes as us publicans.

Their argument is that God has put all earthly religious authority, all wisdom about ultimate reality, into their hands, but this argument remains formal rather than empirical. If one looks at the empirical data, the historical facts of any religious tradition, West or East, one finds numerous things all too human. The only certain conclusion is that this tradition, its leaders and institutions, has been no substitute for God, no unquestionable vicar or vicegerent.

The gap between God and even the best of those who have represented God, governed and taught in God's name, is infinite, as the wisest of such teachers themselves have stressed. God is never the subject of a creature. God never comes under our control. Always, God is the first and the last, subject only to the divine counsels. It is shocking when supposedly religious leaders forget this elementary truth, this entailment of the first Mosaic commandment. We expect those preaching to us, claiming high authority, to know the first lessons of the catechism. When they do not, we are right to suspect both a mediocre mind and a strong will to power — a self-importance or self-assertion so preoccupying that it makes their practice ungodly, heretical.

This happens again and again in the history of religions, so wise people get used to it. Getting used to it, they learn to look to what people do more than what they say. Sometimes fatuous leaders are good-hearted in practice; sometimes they are not. The most pious-appearing leaders can turn bloodthirsty when religious passions arise. Recently the Muslim world has shown us the worst lessons in this phenomenon, but Christians, Jews, and Hindus have no cause for boasting. For example, in trying to defend genocide, Serbian Orthodox leaders have scraped the bottom of the barrel. In appearing to try to forge an alliance with fundamentalist Muslim regimes to defeat population controls, Vatican officials have been nearly as despicable. The faces of Orthodox Jews contorted with hatred of Palestinian Muslims and Christians are object lessons in what the Torah cannot generate if we are to consider it the word of God. The rampages of militant Hindus against Muslim shrines in India deny their having any connection to Gandhian wisdom reposing in *ahimsa* (noninjury). Religious wisdom therefore has good grounds for looking to performance rather than profession of ideals or claims to holiness. Religious people are as religious people do. Fortunately, the saints pass this test with flying colors, as do numerous less noted believers who salt the earth.

WORSHIP

Suppose that the end of wisdom is worship of God. The logic of this supposition might run as follows: wisdom is right order, dealing with things, the components of creation, as they actually are; but God is the source, the linchpin, of right order because God is the source of creation, the Creator; further, this primacy of God stirs an awareness of holiness — reality so pure, so good, that the only proper response is to bow low in awe and praise; therefore, the end, the consummation, the action to which religious wisdom leads, is worship — awe and praise offered to God for the unique divine being and goodness.

Few people fall to their knees because of logic. Many religious people become wise only after years of worship. Wisdom and worship need not stand in a linear relationship: first wisdom, then worship. Usually their relationship is dialectical, moves back and forth. However, both actions or realities emphasize the primacy of God. Religious wisdom agrees with prayer that God alone is the pearl of great price. When we accept the notion, the reality, of God, everything else changes. Our work, our recreation, our money, our friends, our health, our children all beg alignment with a new master, divinity. We cannot work our seventy-hour week as we used to, before the preeminent reality of God crashed in, because now work, success in our career, can be at best a penultimate good. Indeed, now we have to consider the wisdom of observing a Sabbath — one day of the week when we abstain from work, so as to proclaim that our first loyalty is to God. Similar realignments, reassessments, lie in wait for us concerning our recreation, our family life, how we see the future. Whereas previously we had prescinded from our mortality, distracted ourselves from death, now we find many reasons for thinking about death. Whereas once we might have thought the notion of heaven childish, now we realize that it matches up with our deepest passions.

Worship allows us to bring these matters, and everything else on our minds, in our hearts, to God. Certainly, the focus of healthy worship, the best prayer, falls on God, not ourselves, not even our legitimate needs. God accommodates the divine perfection to our needs, may even enjoy helping us, but it is well for us to let our self-concern decrease, our awe and praise of God increase. So in the best of cases we bring all that we are, as individuals and communities, and place it before God to reassert our faith in God, our loyalty to God. Then we clear our gifts away. Better than anything that may bog us down in our own concerns is prayer like that of the Shema, the Gloria, the Te Deum. Such prayer stresses the divine side of the covenant that worship puts in play. It does not deny that God is God-for-us, nor that all our thoughts and emotions about God reflect our human limitations, but it does second, agree to, the movement in our deepest spirits to go out to God for God's own sake.

Something deep in us wants to give the divine splendor its due. Something quintessential wants to praise God purely, beyond any concerns of our own. Secure in heaven, the saints may pray this way constantly, joining the cherubim and seraphim. Indeed, any people for whom God has become fully real stand on the brink of such worship.

The enemy of proper worship is what keeps God from being fully real for us. When we analyze this proposition, we find that the enemy is legion. For example, the mass media — newspapers, television, and the like — present what has happened recently as though God were not necessary, played no role in any news. Superficial and ephemeral (preoccupied with the moment, uninterested in the long view), journalists and entertainers strengthen our tendencies to distraction, the laziness that keeps us from thinking our way through the deep issues with which human existence confronts us.

Another enemy of proper worship is the spate of books on self-help that try to justify our narcissism. Thomas Moore's best-sellers come to mind, but many other authors have pitched in. For most of them, reality shrinks to what gives the reader pain or pleasure. Moore, for instance, has no political interests, no outreach to victims of AIDS or African children starving. He stays far away from suffering, disease, and death, lest the shallowness of his nostrums become apparent. If books such as his came on the market with honest self-descriptions (worldly advice for self-absorbed yuppies), people serious about religious wisdom and worship would have no great quarrel with them. When they are advertised as "classics" of spirituality, any well-educated person has to groan. Compared to the giants of the religious traditions West and East, such psychologically based authors are pathetically superficial. The great reality of God escapes them, and with it goes the profound wonder that anything should be. In their hands religion becomes a subset of how we human beings talk to ourselves, trying to make a world tame enough to let us sleep at night. The new guru is not the desert ascetic, tested through bouts of fasting and dark prayer, but the divorced therapist, good at getting people to talk about themselves.

For the religious person, we get most of our interest, our allure, from our being images of God. How we handle the staple challenges of human maturation — work, love, sex, parenting, mortality — makes us intriguing. What we say to the aging face in the mirror, how men convince themselves that they need a gold chain or women decide to take a few more tranquilizers, is not in itself interesting. It becomes interesting, something that an artist might develop into an absorbing play, when we see the alternatives. What were the steps by which this man descended into narcissism, great concern about his looks? How did this woman get hooked on Valium, or lying, or younger men? Tragedy is as near as the ruined life in the apartment next-door, the whacked-out thirty-year-old child of our friend. Comedy is as rare as profound worship, liturgical hours sung day after day with joy. All is well that ends well, in resurrection and glorification. All that avoids death, resurrection, and glorification is superficial, disordered, half the way to a tragic ending.

So, if you want to live with God successfully, set your heart upon worship. If you want your life to be maximally meaningful, bow low and get some calluses on your knees. Take comfort in the fact that your path, though senseless to the majority of your contemporaries, is the way of the religious masters. Do not become puffed up about this. Remember your many sins and flaws of character. But also do not deny or repress your joy. God is beckoning you to come forth from darkness into ineffable light. The morning stars are coming together for choir practice. Though this slay you, yet must you keep trying to trust it. The divine mystery never leaves. There is no other way to the fully good life than by dealing with it, struggling with the sovereignty it holds, at the end of the day acknowledging with delight that it is always greater, worthy of all honor, praise, and glory.